ultimate
Italian
recipes

Publications International, Ltd.

Favorite Brand Name Recipes at www.fbnr.com

Pictured on the front cover: Lasagna Florentine *(page 203).*
Pictured on the front jacket flap: Spinach & Roasted Pepper Panini *(page 78).*
Pictured on the back cover: Tomato and Caper Crostini *(page 14).*

ISBN-13: 978-1-4127-2707-5
ISBN-10: 1-4127-2707-3

Library of Congress Control Number: 2007932077

Manufactured in China.

8 7 6 5 4 3 2 1

Microwave Cooking: Microwave ovens vary in wattage. Use the cooking times as guidelines and check for doneness before adding more time.

Table of Contents

Antipasto

Favorites

marinated antipasto

¼ cup extra-virgin olive oil
2 tablespoons balsamic vinegar
1 clove garlic, minced
½ teaspoon sugar
½ teaspoon salt
¼ teaspoon black pepper
1 pint (2 cups) cherry tomatoes
1 can (14 ounces) quartered artichoke hearts, drained
8 ounces small balls or cubes fresh mozzarella cheese
1 cup drained whole pitted kalamata olives
¼ cup julienned or chopped fresh basil
   Lettuce leaves

1. Whisk together oil, vinegar, garlic, sugar, salt and pepper in medium bowl.

2. Add tomatoes, artichokes, mozzarella, olives and basil; toss to coat.

3. Let stand at least 30 minutes or cover and chill up to 4 hours (let stand 15 to 30 minutes before serving).

4. Line platter with lettuce leaves; arrange tomato mixture over leaves. Serve at room temperature.

Makes about 5 cups (12 appetizer servings)

Serving Suggestion: Serve antipasto with toothpicks as an appetizer or spoon over Bibb lettuce leaves for a first-course salad.

bruschetta

Nonstick cooking spray
1 cup thinly sliced onion
$\frac{1}{2}$ cup chopped seeded tomato
2 tablespoons capers, drained
$\frac{1}{4}$ teaspoon black pepper
3 cloves garlic, finely chopped
1 teaspoon olive oil
4 slices French bread
$\frac{1}{2}$ cup (2 ounces) shredded Monterey Jack cheese

1. Spray large nonstick skillet with cooking spray. Cook and stir onion over medium heat 5 minutes. Stir in tomato, capers and pepper. Cook 3 minutes.

2. Preheat broiler. Combine garlic and olive oil in small bowl. Brush bread slices with oil mixture. Top with onion mixture; sprinkle with cheese. Place on baking sheet. Broil 3 minutes or until cheese melts.

Makes 4 servings

olive tapenade dip

1½ cups (10-ounce jar) pitted kalamata olives, drained
3 tablespoons olive oil
3 tablespoons *French's®* Spicy Brown Mustard
1 tablespoon minced fresh rosemary leaves *or* 1 teaspoon
      dried rosemary leaves
1 teaspoon minced garlic

1. Place all ingredients in food processor. Process until puréed.

2. Serve with vegetable crudités or pita chips.

Makes 4 (¼-cup) servings

Tip: To pit olives, place in plastic bag. Gently tap with wooden mallet or rolling pin until olives split open. Remove pits.

best pesto

2 cups fresh basil leaves
¼ cup pine nuts
¼ cup olive oil
3 cloves garlic, finely chopped or pressed
¼ teaspoon salt
½ cup grated Parmesan or Romano cheese

1. Place basil, nuts, oil, garlic and salt in food processor or blender container. Process on high until a spreadable consistency is reached. Stir in cheese.

2. Serve on pasta, crackers or stir into pasta sauces. Pesto can be stored in refrigerator up to 2 weeks.   *Makes about 1½ cups*

eggplant rolls

1 large eggplant (about 1¼ pounds)
3 tablespoons extra-virgin olive oil
  Salt and black pepper
1 cup ricotta cheese
½ cup grated Asiago cheese
¼ cup julienned or chopped sun-dried tomatoes packed in oil
¼ cup chopped fresh basil or Italian parsley
⅛ teaspoon red pepper flakes
  Cherry tomatoes, halved (optional)
  Fresh thyme sprigs or basil leaves (optional)

1. Preheat broiler.

2. Trim off stem end from eggplant; peel eggplant, if desired. Cut eggplant lengthwise into 6 long, thin slices about ¼ inch thick. Brush both sides of eggplant slices with oil; sprinkle with salt and pepper to taste. Place on rack of broiler pan.

3. Broil eggplant 4 inches from heat source 4 to 5 minutes per side or until golden brown and slightly softened. Let eggplant cool to room temperature.

4. Combine ricotta cheese, Asiago cheese, sun-dried tomatoes, basil and red pepper flakes in small bowl; mix well. Spread mixture evenly over cooled eggplant slices. Roll up and cut each roll in half diagonally.

5. Arrange seam side down on serving platter; garnish with tomatoes and thyme sprig.   *Makes 6 appetizer servings*

peperonata

1 tablespoon extra-virgin olive oil
4 large red, yellow or orange bell peppers, cut into thin strips
2 cloves garlic, coarsely chopped
12 pimiento-stuffed green olives or pitted black olives, cut into halves
2 to 3 tablespoons white wine vinegar or red wine vinegar
1/4 teaspoon salt
1/4 teaspoon black pepper

1. Heat olive oil in 12-inch skillet over medium-high heat. Add bell peppers; cook and stir 8 to 9 minutes or until edges begin to brown, stirring frequently.

2. Reduce heat to medium. Add garlic; cook and stir 1 to 2 minutes. *Do not allow garlic to brown.* Add olives, vinegar, salt and black pepper. Cook 1 to 2 minutes or until all liquid has evaporated.   *Makes 4 to 5 servings*

Traditionally, peperonata is served hot as a condiment or side dish with meat dishes. It complements both chicken and pork. Or, it can be chilled and served as part of an antipasti selection.

tomato and caper crostini

1 French roll, cut into 8 slices
2 plum tomatoes, finely chopped
1 tablespoon plus 1$\frac{1}{2}$ teaspoons capers, drained
1$\frac{1}{2}$ teaspoons dried basil
1 teaspoon extra-virgin olive oil
1 ounce crumbled feta cheese with sun-dried tomatoes and basil, or any variety

1. Preheat oven to 350°F.

2. Place bread slices on ungreased baking sheet in single layer. Bake 15 minutes or just until golden brown. Cool completely.

3. Meanwhile, combine tomatoes, capers, basil and oil in small bowl; mix well.

4. Just before serving, spoon tomato mixture on each bread slice; sprinkle with cheese. *Makes 4 servings*

margherita panini bites

1 loaf (16 ounces) ciabatta or crusty Italian bread, cut into
    16 ($\frac{1}{2}$-inch) slices
8 teaspoons prepared pesto
16 fresh basil leaves
8 slices (1 ounce each) mozzarella cheese
24 thin slices plum tomatoes (about 2 large tomatoes)
    Olive oil

1. Preheat indoor grill. Spread each of 8 slices bread with 1 teaspoon pesto.
Top each slice with 2 basil leaves, 1 slice mozzarella cheese and 3 tomato
slices. Top with remaining bread slices.

2. Brush both sides of sandwiches lightly with olive oil. Cook sandwiches
5 minutes or until lightly browned and cheese is melted.

3. Cut each sandwich into 4 pieces. Serve warm.

Makes 32 panini bites

Panini are fancy grilled cheese sandwiches usually made
on a indoor electric grill with ridges or a ridged grill pan.
The sandwiches are pressed together as they are heating
and melting the cheese. The Margherita panini, named after
Queen Margherita, is made with tomato (red), cheese (white)
and basil (green), the colors of the Italian flag.

sicilian caponata

5 tablespoons olive or vegetable oil, divided
8 cups (1½ pounds) cubed unpeeled eggplant
2½ cups onion slices
1 cup chopped celery
1 can (14½ ounces) CONTADINA® Recipe Ready Diced Tomatoes
    with Roasted Garlic, undrained
⅓ cup chopped pitted ripe olives, drained
¼ cup balsamic or red wine vinegar
2 tablespoons capers
2 teaspoons granulated sugar
½ teaspoon salt
Dash of black pepper

1. Heat 3 tablespoons oil in large skillet. Add eggplant; sauté 6 minutes. Remove eggplant from skillet.

2. Heat remaining 2 tablespoons oil in same skillet. Add onions and celery; sauté 5 minutes or until vegetables are tender.

3. Stir in undrained tomatoes and eggplant; cover. Simmer 15 minutes or until eggplant is tender.

4. Stir in olives, vinegar, capers, sugar, salt and pepper; simmer, uncovered, 5 minutes, stirring occasionally. Serve with toasted bread slices, if desired.

Makes 4½ cups caponata

For a festive presentation, hollow out half of a small eggplant and fill it with the caponata. Place it on a serving platter with the toasted bread slices and garnish as desired.

tuscan white bean crostini

2 cans (about 15 ounces each) white beans (such as cannellini
    or Great Northern), rinsed and drained
$^1/_2$ large red bell pepper, finely chopped *or* $^1/_3$ cup finely chopped
    roasted red bell pepper
$^1/_3$ cup finely chopped onion
$^1/_3$ cup red wine vinegar
3 tablespoons chopped fresh parsley
1 tablespoon olive oil
2 cloves garlic, minced
$^1/_2$ teaspoon dried oregano
$^1/_4$ teaspoon black pepper
18 slices French bread, about $^1/_4$ inch thick

1. Combine beans, bell pepper and onion in large bowl.

2. Whisk together vinegar, parsley, oil, garlic, oregano and black pepper in
small bowl. Pour over bean mixture; toss to coat. Cover; refrigerate 2 hours
or overnight.

3. Arrange bread slices in single layer on large ungreased baking sheet or
broiler pan. Broil, 6 to 8 inches from heat, 30 to 45 seconds or until bread
slices are lightly toasted. Cool completely.

4. Top each toasted bread slice with about 3 tablespoons bean mixture.

Makes 6 servings

onion and pepper calzones

  1 teaspoon vegetable oil
$\frac{1}{2}$ cup chopped onion
$\frac{1}{2}$ cup chopped green bell pepper
$\frac{1}{4}$ teaspoon salt
$\frac{1}{8}$ teaspoon dried basil
$\frac{1}{8}$ teaspoon dried oregano
$\frac{1}{8}$ teaspoon black pepper
  1 can (12 ounces) refrigerated biscuit dough (10 biscuits)
$\frac{1}{4}$ cup (1 ounce) shredded mozzarella cheese
$\frac{1}{2}$ cup prepared pasta or pizza sauce
  2 tablespoons grated Parmesan cheese

1. Preheat oven to 400°F. Heat oil in medium nonstick skillet over medium heat. Add onion and bell pepper; cook 5 minutes or until tender, stirring occasionally. Remove from heat. Add salt, basil, oregano and black pepper; stir until blended. Remove from heat; cool slightly.

2. Meanwhile, flatten biscuits into $3\frac{1}{2}$-inch circles about $\frac{1}{8}$ inch thick using palm of hand.

3. Stir mozzarella cheese into onion mixture. Spoon 1 teaspoon onion mixture onto each biscuit. Fold biscuits in half, covering filling. Press edges with tines of fork to seal; transfer to ungreased baking sheet.

4. Bake 10 to 12 minutes or until golden brown. Meanwhile, place pasta sauce in small microwavable bowl. Cover with vented plastic wrap. Microwave on HIGH 3 minutes or until hot.

5. To serve, spoon pasta sauce and Parmesan cheese evenly over each calzone. Serve immediately. *Makes 10 appetizers*

skewered antipasto

1 jar (8 ounces) SONOMA® Marinated Dried Tomatoes
1 pound (3 medium) new potatoes, cooked until tender
2 cups bite-sized vegetable pieces (such as celery, bell peppers,
   radishes, carrots, cucumber and green onions)
1 cup drained cooked egg tortellini and/or spinach tortellini
1 tablespoon chopped fresh chives *or* 1 teaspoon dried chives
1 tablespoon chopped fresh rosemary leaves *or* 1 teaspoon
   dried rosemary

Drain oil from tomatoes into medium bowl. Place tomatoes in small bowl;
set aside. Cut potatoes into 1-inch cubes. Add potatoes, vegetables,
tortellini, chives and rosemary to oil in medium bowl. Stir to coat with oil;
cover and marinate 1 hour at room temperature. To assemble, alternately
thread tomatoes, potatoes, vegetables and tortellini onto 6-inch skewers.

Makes 12 to 14 skewers

asparagus & prosciutto antipasto

12 fresh asparagus spears (about 8 ounces)
 2 ounces cream cheese, softened
 $1/4$ cup crumbled blue cheese or goat cheese
 $1/4$ teaspoon black pepper
 1 package (3 to 4 ounces) thinly sliced prosciutto

1. Trim off and discard bottom 2 inches of asparagus spears. Simmer
asparagus in salted water in large skillet 4 to 5 minutes or until crisp-tender.
Drain; immediately immerse in cold water to stop cooking. Drain; pat dry.

2. Combine cheeses and pepper in small bowl; mix well. Cut prosciutto
slices in half crosswise to make 12 pieces. Spread cream cheese mixture
evenly over one side of each prosciutto piece. Wrap each asparagus spear
with one piece of prosciutto. Serve at room temperature or slightly chilled.

Makes 6 servings

arugula-prosciutto wrapped breadsticks with garlic mustard sauce

1/2 cup mayonnaise

6 tablespoons grated Parmesan cheese

2 tablespoons *French's®* Honey Dijon Mustard

1 tablespoon chopped fresh basil

2 teaspoons minced garlic

1 package (4 1/2 ounces) long breadsticks (12 to 16 breadsticks)

1 1/3 cups *French's®* French Fried Onions, crushed

1/2 pound thinly sliced prosciutto or smoked deli ham

1 bunch arugula (about 20 leaves) or green leaf lettuce, washed, drained and stems removed

1. Combine mayonnaise, cheese, mustard, basil and garlic in mixing bowl. Spread half of each breadstick with some of mustard sauce. Roll in French Fried Onions, pressing firmly.

2. Arrange prosciutto slices on flat work surface. Top each slice with leaf of arugula. Place coated end of breadsticks on top; roll up jelly-roll style. Place seam side down on serving platter.

3. Serve wrapped breadsticks with remaining mustard sauce for dipping.

Makes 16 appetizers

onion & white bean spread

1 can (about 15 ounces) cannellini or Great Northern beans, rinsed and drained
2 cloves garlic, minced
¼ cup minced green onion
¼ cup grated Parmesan cheese
¼ cup olive oil
1 tablespoon fresh rosemary leaves, finely chopped
French bread slices

1. Combine all ingredients except bread slices in food processor. Process 30 to 40 seconds or until mixture is almost smooth.

2. Spoon bean mixture into serving bowl. Drizzle additional olive oil over spread just before serving. Serve with French bread slices.

Makes 1¼ cups spread

For a more rustic spread, place all ingredients in a medium bowl and mash with a potato masher.

Soups and *Salads*

hearty bean & pasta soup

1 cup uncooked elbow macaroni

2 tablespoons olive oil

1 medium onion, chopped

2 cloves garlic, minced

4 cups water

2 cans (about 14 ounces each) chicken or vegetable broth

1 jar (26 ounces) marinara sauce

1 can (about 15 ounces) Great Northern or cannellini beans, rinsed and drained

2 teaspoons balsamic vinegar

1 pound fresh spinach, chopped

$1/2$ cup grated Parmesan cheese (optional)

1. Cook macaroni according to package directions; drain.

2. Meanwhile, heat oil in Dutch oven or large saucepan over medium heat. Add onion and garlic; cook and stir 5 minutes or until onion is tender.

3. Stir in water, broth, marinara sauce and beans; bring to a boil. Reduce heat to low; cook, uncovered, 10 minutes, stirring occasionally. Stir in vinegar, then spinach and cooked pasta; cook 5 minutes. Sprinkle with cheese before serving. *Makes 10 to 12 servings*

spinach & prosciutto salad

Salad

    12 slices of prosciutto

    6 small plum tomatoes

    4 tablespoons FILIPPO BERIO® Extra-Virgin Olive Oil

    Freshly ground black pepper

    7 ounces of baby spinach leaves, washed and dried well

    7 ounces of baby fresh asparagus, blanched for two minutes and
       chilled

Dressing

    2 tablespoons FILIPPO BERIO® Extra-Virgin Olive Oil

    2 tablespoons fresh lemon juice

    2 tablespoons finely shredded fresh basil

    A little sugar to taste

    Parmesan shavings, for garnish

Preheat the oven to 350°F. Put the prosciutto and tomatoes cut side up
onto a baking tray. Drizzle with the olive oil and season well. Cook for
25 minutes or until just soft. Arrange the spinach and asparagus onto the
serving plates and top with the tomatoes and prosciutto. Mix the salad
dressing ingredients together and season to taste. Pour over the salad just
before serving. *Makes 4 servings*

italian antipasto salad

1 box (9 ounces) BIRDS EYE® frozen Deluxe Artichoke Heart Halves
1 box (9 ounces) BIRDS EYE® frozen Deluxe Whole Green Beans
12 lettuce leaves
1 pound salami, cut into $3/4$-inch cubes
$3/4$ pound provolone cheese, cut into $3/4$-inch cubes
1 jar (7 ounces) roasted red peppers*
$1/3$ cup Italian salad dressing

*Or, substitute pimientos, drained and cut into thin strips.

• In large saucepan, cook artichokes and green beans according to package directions; drain. Rinse under cold water to cool; drain again.

• Place lettuce on serving platter. Arrange cooked vegetables, salami, cheese and peppers in separate piles.

• Drizzle with dressing just before serving.   *Makes 6 servings*

Serving Suggestion: **Add pitted ripe olives and jarred peperoncini, if desired.**

Birds Eye Idea: **Don't discard the water after boiling vegetables. Use it for making soups, sauces or rice dishes to keep precious nutrients.**

pasta fagioli soup

2 cans (about 14 ounces each) beef or vegetable broth
1 can (about 15 ounces) Great Northern beans, rinsed and drained
1 can (about 14 ounces) diced tomatoes
2 medium zucchini, quartered lengthwise and sliced
1 tablespoon olive oil
1½ teaspoons minced garlic
½ teaspoon dried basil
½ teaspoon dried oregano
½ cup uncooked tubetti, ditali or small shell pasta
½ cup garlic seasoned croutons
½ cup grated Asiago or Romano cheese
3 tablespoons chopped fresh basil or Italian parsley (optional)

Slow Cooker Directions

1. Combine broth, beans, tomatoes, zucchini, oil, garlic, dried basil and oregano in slow cooker; mix well. Cover; cook on LOW 3 to 4 hours.

2. Stir in pasta. Cover; cook on LOW 1 hour or until pasta is tender.

3. Serve soup with croutons and cheese. Garnish with fresh basil.

Makes 5 to 6 servings

Only small pasta varieties like tubetti, ditali or small shell pasta should be used in this recipe. The low heat of a slow cooker won't allow larger pasta shapes to cook completely.

rigatoni salad

12 ounces rigatoni, cooked and drained
1 to 2 cups chopped greens, such as arugula, frisée or any crisp lettuce
1 package (10 ounces) frozen snow peas or sugar snap peas, thawed
8 ounces cherry tomatoes, cut into halves
1 medium red or yellow bell pepper, cut into thin strips
$\frac{1}{2}$ red onion, cut into thin strips
$\frac{1}{3}$ cup sliced black olives
$\frac{1}{3}$ to $\frac{1}{2}$ cup Italian salad dressing
Grated Parmesan cheese (optional)

Combine all ingredients except cheese in large serving bowl. Toss gently to coat all ingredients. Sprinkle with cheese. *Makes about 8 servings*

tuna and bean salad

1 can (8 ounces) broad or lima beans, rinsed and drained
1 can (about 15 ounces) cannellini beans, rinsed and drained
$\frac{1}{2}$ red onion, thinly sliced
2 cans ($6\frac{1}{2}$ ounces each) tuna in oil, undrained
$\frac{1}{3}$ cup olive or vegetable oil
2 tablespoons red wine vinegar
Black pepper
$\frac{1}{2}$ cup pitted ripe olives
2 tablespoons chopped fresh parsley

1. Combine beans and onion in large bowl. Add tuna; break into large flakes. Blend oil, vinegar and pepper in small bowl; pour over tuna mixture. Add olives and parsley; toss to mix well.

2. Spoon onto individual serving plates. *Makes 6 servings*

panzanella (italian bread salad)

4 ounces day-old French bread, cubed*
4 plum tomatoes, chopped
3 tablespoons extra-virgin olive oil
2 tablespoons red wine vinegar
1 clove garlic, minced
$1/2$ teaspoon salt
$1/4$ cup chopped fresh basil

Substitute day-old whole wheat bread, sourdough bread or pita bread for the Italian bread. Cube it or tear it into small pieces.

1. Combine bread cubes and tomatoes in medium serving bowl.

2. Whisk together oil, vinegar, garlic and salt in small bowl; stir in basil. Pour over bread mixture; toss until well mixed. *Makes 6 servings*

italian bean and tomato soup

1 can (about 16 ounces) kidney beans, drained
1 can (about 16 ounces) white cannellini beans, drained
1 can (about 15 ounces) Italian stewed tomatoes, undrained
1 can (about 14 ounces) ready-to-serve chicken broth
$1/2$ cup small pasta shells (uncooked)
Fresh mushrooms, sliced

In a medium saucepan, combine kidney and cannellini beans, tomatoes, chicken broth and pasta shells. Bring to a boil. Reduce heat and simmer, covered, until pasta is cooked, about 10 minutes. Serve with grated Parmesan cheese and garnish with parsley, if desired. Serve with fresh mushrooms. *Makes about $6^1/2$ cups*

Favorite recipe from **Mushroom Council**

italian beef and barley soup

1 boneless beef top sirloin steak (about 1½ pounds)
1 tablespoon vegetable oil
4 medium carrots or parsnips, cut into ¼-inch slices
1 cup chopped onion
1 teaspoon dried thyme
½ teaspoon dried rosemary
¼ teaspoon black pepper
⅓ cup uncooked pearl barley
2 cans (about 14 ounces each) beef broth
1 can (about 14 ounces) diced tomatoes with Italian seasoning

Slow Cooker Directions

1. Cut beef into 1-inch pieces. Heat oil over medium-high heat in large skillet. Brown beef on all sides; set aside.

2. Place carrots and onion in slow cooker; sprinkle with thyme, rosemary and pepper. Top with barley and beef. Pour broth and tomatoes over meat.

3. Cover; cook on LOW 8 to 10 hours or until beef is tender.

Makes 6 servings

Choose pearl barley rather than quick-cooking barley because it will stand up to long cooking.

tomato-fresh mozzarella salad

Vinaigrette Dressing (recipe follows)
1 pound fresh mozzarella cheese
1 pound ripe tomatoes
Fresh basil leaves
Salt and black pepper

1. Prepare Vinaigrette Dressing.

2. Cut mozzarella into $1/4$-inch slices. Cut tomatoes into $1/4$-inch slices. Arrange mozzarella slices, tomato slices and basil leaves overlapping on plate.

3. Drizzle with dressing. Sprinkle with salt and pepper.

Makes 4 servings

vinaigrette dressing

1 tablespoon balsamic vinegar or red wine vinegar
$1/4$ teaspoon Dijon mustard
Pinch *each* sugar, salt and black pepper
$1/4$ cup extra-virgin olive oil

1. Combine vinegar, mustard, sugar, salt and pepper in small bowl; whisk until smooth. Add oil in thin stream, whisking until mixture is smooth.

2. Refrigerate until ready to use. Whisk again before serving.

Makes about $1/4$ cup dressing

roasted pepper and avocado salad

2 red bell peppers
2 orange bell peppers
2 yellow bell peppers
2 ripe avocados, halved, pitted and peeled
3 shallots, thinly sliced
¼ cup FILIPPO BERIO® Extra Virgin Olive Oil
1 clove garlic, crushed
Finely grated peel and juice of 1 lemon
Salt and freshly ground black pepper

Place bell peppers on baking sheet. Broil, 4 to 5 inches from heat, 5 minutes on each side or until entire surface of each bell pepper is blistered and blackened slightly. Place bell peppers in paper bag. Close bag; cool 15 to 20 minutes. Cut around cores of bell peppers; twist and remove. Cut bell peppers lengthwise in half. Peel off skin with paring knife; rinse under cold water to remove seeds. Slice bell peppers into ½-inch-thick strips; place in shallow dish. Cut avocados into ¼-inch-thick slices; add to bell peppers. Sprinkle with shallots.

In small bowl, whisk together olive oil, garlic, lemon peel and juice. Pour over bell pepper mixture. Cover; refrigerate at least 1 hour before serving. Season to taste with salt and black pepper.   *Makes 6 servings*

hearty tortellini soup

1 small red onion, chopped
2 medium carrots, chopped
2 ribs celery, thinly sliced
1 small zucchini, chopped
2 plum tomatoes, chopped
2 cloves garlic, minced
2 cans (14$\frac{1}{2}$ ounces each) chicken broth
1 can (15 to 19 ounces) red kidney beans, rinsed and drained
2 tablespoons _French's_® Worcestershire Sauce
1 package (9 ounces) refrigerated tortellini pasta

1. Heat _2 tablespoons oil_ in 6-quart saucepot or Dutch oven over medium-high heat. Add vegetables, tomatoes and garlic. Cook and stir 5 minutes or until vegetables are crisp-tender.

2. Add broth, _½ cup water,_ beans and Worcestershire. Heat to boiling. Stir in pasta. Return to boiling. Cook 5 minutes or until pasta is tender, stirring occasionally. Serve with crusty bread and grated Parmesan cheese, if desired.

Makes 4 servings

Tortellini are small pasta nuggets stuffed with various fillings ranging from cheese and vegetables to meats. They are folded over and shaped into a ring or hat. Premade refrigerated or frozen stuffed tortellini are widely available.

italian artichoke and rotini salad

4 ounces uncooked whole wheat or tricolored rotini
1 can (14 ounces) quartered artichoke hearts, drained
$\frac{1}{2}$ cup (4 ounces) sliced pimientos
1 can ($2\frac{1}{2}$ ounces) sliced black olives, drained
2 tablespoons finely chopped onion
2 teaspoons dried basil
$\frac{1}{2}$ clove garlic, minced
$\frac{1}{8}$ teaspoon black pepper
3 tablespoons cider vinegar
1 tablespoon extra-virgin olive oil
$\frac{1}{4}$ teaspoon salt

1. Cook rotini according to package directions.

2. Meanwhile, combine artichokes, pimientos, olives, onion, basil, garlic and pepper in large bowl.

3. Drain pasta; rinse under cold running water to cool completely. Drain well. Add pasta to artichoke mixture; toss to blend.

4. Just before serving, combine vinegar, oil and salt; whisk until well blended. Toss with pasta mixture to coat.   *Makes 6 servings*

marinated tomato salad

2 cups cherry tomatoes, cut into halves
1 large cucumber, cut in half lengthwise and sliced
1 large yellow or red bell pepper, cut into strips
3 slices red onion, quartered
2 tablespoons balsamic vinegar
1 tablespoon olive oil
$\frac{1}{2}$ teaspoon dried basil
$\frac{1}{4}$ to $\frac{1}{2}$ teaspoon onion salt
$\frac{1}{4}$ teaspoon garlic powder
$\frac{1}{4}$ teaspoon dried oregano

1. Combine tomatoes, cucumber, pepper and onion in large bowl.

2. Combine vinegar, oil, basil, onion salt, garlic powder and oregano in small bowl. Pour over vegetables; mix well. Let stand at room temperature 15 to 30 minutes. *Makes 6 to 8 servings*

tuscan bread salad (panzanella salad)

$1\frac{1}{2}$ pounds tomatoes, chopped (about 4 large)
1 cucumber, peeled and chopped
1 small red onion, thinly sliced
1 cup WISH-BONE® Italian Dressing
3 tablespoons drained capers
4 cups day-old, cubed Italian bread (about 6 ounces)

In large bowl, combine all ingredients except bread. Add bread and toss until evenly coated. Chill at least 1 hour before serving.

Makes 9 (1-cup) servings

Pizza, Panini

and Breads

plum tomato basil pizza

1 cup (4 ounces) shredded mozzarella cheese
1 (10-ounce) package prepared pizza crust
4 ripe seeded Italian plum tomatoes, sliced
$\frac{1}{2}$ cup fresh basil leaves
$1\frac{1}{2}$ teaspoons TABASCO® brand Pepper Sauce
    Olive oil

Preheat oven to 425°F. Sprinkle shredded mozzarella cheese evenly over pizza crust. Layer with tomatoes and basil. Drizzle with TABASCO® Sauce and olive oil. Bake on pizza pan or stone 15 minutes or until cheese is melted and crust is golden brown.

Makes 4 servings

panini with prosciutto, mozzarella and ripe olives

1 cup California ripe olives, sliced
$\frac{1}{4}$ cup chopped fresh basil
8 wedges prepared herb focaccia
$\frac{1}{3}$ cup coarse mustard
1 pound prosciutto, sliced
24 ounces mozzarella, thinly sliced
4 cups arugula, washed, dried

Combine sliced olives and basil in bowl; mix well. Slice each focaccia wedge horizontally in half. Spread cut sides of each wedge with 1 teaspoon mustard. Layer bottom halves with 2 tablespoons olive mixture, 2 ounces prosciutto, 3 ounces mozzarella and $\frac{1}{2}$ cup arugula. Top with remaining focaccia halves.

Makes 8 servings

Favorite recipe from California Olive Industry

italian bistro tart

1 pound puff pastry (12-inch)
$1/2$ pound lean bacon, cooked and diced
5 medium yellow onions, sliced thinly
2 tablespoons butter
1 egg
$3/4$ cup heavy cream
1 teaspoon garlic salt
2 ounces Swiss cheese, grated

Roll puff pastry into 14-inch circle, $1/8$-inch thick. Place in a tart pan and fill with pie weights. Bake at 350°F for 15 minutes. Remove from oven and let cool. Cook onions in butter over low heat, in covered pan, until soft and tender. Do not brown onions. Spread cooked bacon and onions in pre-baked crust. Beat egg, cream and garlic salt together in medium bowl. Pour over bacon-onion mixture. Sprinkle with cheese. Bake at 350°F for 25 to 30 minutes until golden brown and egg mixture sets. Let stand five minutes before cutting.   *Makes 6 servings.*

Favorite recipe from **National Onion Association**

Pizza, Panini and Breads

tomato-artichoke focaccia

1 package (16 ounces) hot roll mix
2 tablespoons wheat bran
1¼ cups hot water
4 teaspoons olive oil, divided
1 cup thinly sliced onion
2 cloves garlic, minced
1 cup sun-dried tomatoes (4 ounces dry), rehydrated* and
  cut into strips
1 cup artichoke hearts, sliced
1 tablespoon minced fresh rosemary
2 tablespoons freshly grated Parmesan cheese
Fresh rosemary springs

*To rehydrate sun-dried tomatoes, pour 1 cup boiling water over tomatoes in small bowl. Let soak 5 to 10 minutes or until softened; drain well.

1. Preheat oven to 400°F. Combine dry ingredients and contents of yeast packet from hot roll mix in large bowl. Add bran; mix well. Stir in hot water and 2 teaspoons oil. Knead dough about 5 minutes or until ingredients are blended.

2. Spray 15½×11½-inch baking pan or 14-inch pizza pan with nonstick cooking spray. Press dough onto bottom of prepared pan. Cover; let rise 15 minutes.

3. Heat 1 teaspoon oil in medium skillet over low heat. Add onion and garlic; cook and stir 2 to 3 minutes or until onions are tender.

4. Brush surface of dough with remaining teaspoon oil. Top dough with onion mixture, tomatoes, artichokes and fresh rosemary. Sprinkle with Parmesan.

5. Bake 25 to 30 minutes or until lightly browned on top. Cut into 16 squares. Garnish with fresh rosemary sprigs.   *Makes 16 servings*

panini with fresh mozzarella and basil

$\frac{1}{2}$ cup prepared vinaigrette
1 loaf (16 ounces) Italian bread, cut in half lengthwise
6 ounces fresh mozzarella cheese, cut into 12 slices
8 ounces thinly sliced oven-roasted deli turkey
12 to 16 fresh whole basil leaves
1 large tomato, thinly sliced
$\frac{1}{2}$ cup thinly sliced red onion
$\frac{1}{8}$ teaspoon red pepper flakes

1. Preheat indoor grill. Spoon vinaigrette evenly over both cut sides of bread.

2. Arrange cheese evenly over bottom half of bread; top with turkey, basil, tomato and onion. Sprinkle with red pepper flakes. Cover with top half of bread; press down firmly. Cut into 4 sandwiches.

3. Place sandwiches on grill; close lid. Cook 5 to 7 minutes or until cheese melts. *Makes 4 servings*

fast pesto focaccia

1 can (13.8 ounces) refrigerated pizza dough
2 tablespoons prepared pesto
4 sun-dried tomatoes, packed in oil, drained

1. Preheat oven to 425°F. Lightly grease 8-inch square baking pan. Unroll pizza dough. Fold in half; press gently into pan.

2. Spread pesto evenly over dough. Chop tomatoes or snip with kitchen scissors; sprinkle over pesto. Press tomatoes into dough. Using wooden spoon handle, make indentations in dough every 2 inches.

3. Bake 10 to 12 minutes or until golden brown. Cut into 16 squares. Serve warm or at room temperature. *Makes 16 servings*

grilled vegetable panini

1/2 cup mayonnaise

1 jar (6 ounces) marinated artichoke hearts, drained and chopped

2 tablespoons grated Parmesan cheese

1 teaspoon finely minced garlic

2 small zucchini or yellow squash, cut lengthwise into 1/4-inch slices

1 small Japanese eggplant, cut lengthwise into 1/4-inch slices

1 red bell pepper, cut into 1/2-inch strips

Olive oil

8 thick slices round sourdough or Italian bread

8 slices mozzarella cheese

Fresh basil leaves

1. Combine mayonnaise, artichokes, Parmesan cheese and garlic; set aside. Brush zucchini, eggplant and bell pepper with oil.

2. Heat electric grill or large grill pan until hot. Grill vegetables in single layer 3 to 5 minutes until tender. Set aside.

3. Spread mayonnaise mixture on one side of each bread slice. Layer vegetables on 4 slices. Top each with 2 slices cheese and basil, if desired. Cover with remaining bread slices, mayonnaise side down. Grill sandwiches 3 minutes or just until cheese melts. Cut in half to serve.

Makes 4 servings

pesto-parmesan twists

1 loaf (16 ounces) frozen bread dough, thawed
¼ cup prepared pesto sauce
⅔ cup grated Parmesan cheese, divided
1 tablespoon olive oil

1. Line baking sheets with parchment paper. Roll out dough to 20×10-inch rectangle on lightly floured surface.

2. Spread pesto evenly over half of dough; sprinkle with ⅓ cup cheese. Fold remaining half of dough over filling, forming 10-inch square. Roll square into 12×10-inch rectangle. Cut into 12 (1-inch) strips with sharp knife. Cut strips in half crosswise to form 24 strips total.

3. Twist each strip several times; place on prepared baking sheets. Cover with clean kitchen towel or plastic wrap; let rise in warm, draft-free place 20 minutes.

4. Preheat oven to 350°F. Brush breadsticks with oil; sprinkle with remaining ⅓ cup cheese. Bake 16 to 18 minutes or until golden brown.

Makes 24 breadsticks

Pesto is traditionally an uncooked green sauce made with basil and pine nuts either crushed with a mortar and pestle or finely chopped with a food processor. Fresh and prepared pestos are now made with many other ingredients and are perfect served over pasta, with meats and fish and as a spread for breads and sandwiches.

portobello & fontina sandwiches

2 teaspoons olive oil
2 large portobello mushrooms, stems removed
   Salt and black pepper
2 to 3 tablespoons sun-dried tomato pesto
4 slices crusty Italian bread
4 ounces fontina cheese, sliced
$\frac{1}{2}$ cup fresh basil leaves

1. Preheat broiler. Line baking sheet with foil.

2. Drizzle oil over both sides of mushrooms; season with salt and pepper. Place mushrooms, gill sides up, on prepared baking sheet. Broil mushrooms about 4 minutes per side or until tender. Cut into $\frac{1}{4}$-inch-thick slices.

3. Spread pesto evenly on 2 bread slices; layer with mushrooms, cheese and basil. Top with remaining bread slices. Brush outsides of sandwiches lightly with oil.

4. Heat large grill pan or skillet over medium heat until hot. Add sandwiches; press down lightly with spatula or weigh down with small plate. Cook sandwiches 4 to 5 minutes per side or until cheese melts and sandwiches are golden brown.   *Makes 2 sandwiches*

caramelized onion and olive pizza

   2 tablespoons olive oil
1$\frac{1}{2}$ pounds onions, thinly sliced
   2 teaspoons fresh rosemary leaves *or* **1 teaspoon dried rosemary**
  $\frac{1}{4}$ cup water
   1 tablespoon balsamic vinegar
   1 cup California ripe olives, sliced
   1 (12-inch) prebaked thick pizza crust
   2 cups (8 ounces) shredded mozzarella cheese

Heat oil in medium nonstick skillet. Add onions and rosemary. Cook, stirring frequently, until onions begin to brown and browned bits begin to stick to bottom of skillet, about 15 minutes. Stir in $\frac{1}{4}$ cup water; scrape up any browned bits. Reduce heat to medium-low and continue to cook, stirring occasionally, until onions are golden and sweet-tasting, 15 to 30 minutes; add more water, 1 tablespoon at a time, if onion mixture appears dry. Remove pan from heat and stir in vinegar, scraping up any browned bits from pan. Gently stir in olives. Place crust on pizza pan or baking sheet. Spoon onion mixture into center of crust. Sprinkle with cheese. Bake in 450°F oven until cheese is melted and just beginning to brown, about 15 minutes. Cut into wedges and serve warm.   *Makes 8 to 10 servings*

Favorite recipe from **California Olive Industry**

pepperoni-oregano focaccia

1 tablespoon cornmeal
1 package (13.8 ounces) refrigerated pizza crust dough
$^1/_2$ cup finely chopped pepperoni (3 to 3$^1/_2$ ounces)
1$^1/_2$ teaspoons finely chopped fresh oregano *or* **$^1/_2$ teaspoon**
  dried oregano
2 teaspoons extra-virgin olive oil

1. Preheat oven to 425°F. Spray baking sheet with nonstick cooking spray; sprinkle with cornmeal. Set aside.

2. Unroll dough onto lightly floured surface. Pat dough into 12×9-inch rectangle. Sprinkle half the pepperoni and half the oregano over one side of dough. Fold over dough, making 12×4$^1/_2$-inch rectangle.

3. Roll dough into 12×9-inch rectangle. Place on prepared baking sheet. Prick dough with fork at 2-inch intervals about 30 times. Brush with oil; sprinkle with remaining pepperoni and oregano.

4. Bake 12 to 15 minutes or until golden brown. (Prick dough several more times if dough puffs as it bakes.) Cut into strips. *Makes 12 servings*

mozzarella, pesto and fresh tomato panini

8 slices country Italian, sourdough or other firm-textured bread
8 slices SARGENTO® Deli Style Sliced Mozzarella Cheese
$1/3$ cup prepared pesto
8 slices ripe tomato
2 tablespoons olive oil

1. Top each of 4 slices of bread with 1 slice of cheese. Spread pesto over cheese. Top with tomatoes and remaining slices of cheese. Close sandwiches with remaining 4 slices of bread.

2. Brush olive oil lightly over both sides of sandwiches. Cook sandwiches over medium-low coals or in preheated ridged grill pan over medium heat 3 to 4 minutes per side or until bread is toasted and cheese is melted.

Makes 4 servings

three-pepper pizza

1 cup ($1/2$ of 15-ounce can) CONTADINA® Four Cheese Pizza Sauce
1 (12-inch) prepared pre-baked pizza crust
$1 1/2$ cups (6 ounces) shredded mozzarella cheese, divided
$1/2$ each: red, green and yellow bell peppers, sliced into thin rings
2 tablespoons shredded Parmesan cheese
1 tablespoon chopped fresh basil *or* 1 teaspoon dried basil leaves, crushed

1. Spread pizza sauce onto crust to within 1 inch of edge.

2. Sprinkle with 1 cup mozzarella cheese, bell peppers, remaining mozzarella cheese and Parmesan cheese.

3. Bake according to pizza crust package directions or until crust is crisp and cheese is melted. Sprinkle with basil.

Makes 8 servings

caramelized onion focaccia

2 tablespoons plus 1 teaspoon olive oil, divided
4 medium onions, cut in half and thinly sliced
$\frac{1}{2}$ teaspoon salt
2 tablespoons water
1 tablespoon chopped fresh rosemary leaves
$\frac{1}{4}$ teaspoon ground black pepper
1 loaf (16 ounces) frozen bread dough, thawed
1 cup (4 ounces) shredded fontina cheese
$\frac{1}{4}$ cup grated Parmesan cheese

1. Heat 2 tablespoons oil in large skillet over high heat. Add onions and salt; cook about 10 minutes or until onions begin to brown, stirring occasionally. Stir in water. Reduce heat to medium; partially cover and cook about 20 minutes or until onions are deep golden brown, stirring occasionally. Remove from heat; stir in rosemary and pepper. Let cool slightly.

2. Meanwhile, brush 13×9-inch baking pan with remaining 1 teaspoon oil. Roll out dough to 13×9-inch rectangle on lightly floured surface. Transfer dough to prepared pan; cover and let rise in warm, draft-free place 30 minutes.

3. Preheat oven to 375°F. Prick dough all over (about 12 times) with fork. Sprinkle fontina cheese over dough; top with caramelized onions. Sprinkle with Parmesan cheese.

4. Bake 18 to 20 minutes or until golden brown. Remove from pan to wire rack. Cut into pieces; serve warm. *Makes 12 servings*

ham stromboli

1 package (13.8 ounces) refrigerated pizza crust dough
1 tablespoon prepared mustard
½ pound thinly sliced deli ham
1 package (3½ ounces) pepperoni slices
1 teaspoon Italian seasoning
2 cups (8 ounces) shredded mozzarella cheese

1. Preheat oven to 425°F.

2. Unroll pizza dough on greased jelly-roll pan; pat dough into 12-inch square. Spread mustard over dough to within ½ inch of edges. Layer ham slices down center 6 inches of dough, leaving 3-inch border on either side and ½-inch border at top and bottom. Top ham with pepperoni slices. Sprinkle with Italian seasoning and cheese.

3. Fold sides of dough over filling, pinching center seam and ends to seal. Bake 15 to 20 minutes or until lightly browned.   *Makes 6 servings*

A stromboli is a stuffed sandwich usually made with mozzarella and pepperoni, similar to a calzone. To easily make a stuffed sandwich, start with pizza dough, crescent roll dough, pie crust or biscuit dough. Add your favorite fillings for a delicious lunch or snack eaten either hot or cold.

focaccia with dried tomatoes and fontina

1 tablespoon olive oil

1 loaf (1 pound) frozen bread dough, thawed according to package directions

1 jar (8 ounces) SONOMA® Marinated Dried Tomatoes, drained and 2 tablespoons oil reserved

4 cloves garlic, minced

²⁄₃ cup sliced black olives

1 tablespoon dried basil

1 teaspoon dried oregano

1 teaspoon dried rosemary

2 cups grated fontina cheese

Preheat oven to 425°F. Oil 13×9×2-inch baking pan. Roll and stretch dough on lightly floured surface; fit dough into pan.

Combine reserved tomato oil with garlic; brush over dough. Sprinkle olives, basil, oregano and rosemary evenly over dough. Arrange tomatoes on top; cover with cheese.

Bake for 35 to 40 minutes until bread is springy to the touch and golden brown around edges. (Cover loosely with foil during last 10 minutes if becoming too brown.) Cut into squares while still warm.

Makes 16 squares

sausage, peppers & onion pizza

$\frac{1}{2}$ **pound bulk Italian sausage**
1 medium red bell pepper, cut into strips
1 pre-baked pizza crust (14 inches)
1 cup spaghetti or pizza sauce
$1\frac{1}{2}$ **cups shredded mozzarella cheese**
$1\frac{1}{3}$ **cups French's® French Fried Onions**

1. Preheat oven to 450°F. Cook sausage in nonstick skillet over medium heat until browned, stirring frequently; drain. Add bell pepper and cook until crisp-tender, stirring occasionally.

2. Top pizza crust with sauce, sausage mixture and cheese. Bake 8 to 10 minutes or until cheese melts. Sprinkle with French Fried Onions; bake 2 minutes or until onions are golden. *Makes 8 servings*

You can substitute link sausage for the bulk sausage. Just remove the meat from the casing before cooking.

Pizza, Panini and Breads

spinach & roasted pepper panini

1 loaf (12 ounces) focaccia
1½ cups spinach leaves (about 12 leaves)
1 jar (about 7 ounces) roasted red peppers, drained
4 ounces fontina cheese, thinly sliced
¾ cup thinly sliced red onion
Olive oil

1. Place focaccia on cutting board; cut in half horizontally. Layer bottom half with spinach, peppers, cheese and onion. Cover with top half of focaccia. Brush outsides of sandwich very lightly with olive oil. Cut sandwich into 4 equal pieces.

2. Heat large nonstick skillet over medium heat. Add sandwiches; press down lightly with spatula or weigh down with small plate. Cook sandwiches 4 to 5 minutes per side or until cheese melts and sandwiches are golden brown. *Makes 4 servings*

Focaccia can be found in the bakery section of most supermarkets. It is often available in different flavors, such as tomato, herb, cheese or onion.

prosciutto provolone rolls

1 loaf (1 pound) frozen bread dough, thawed
¼ cup garlic and herb spreadable cheese
6 thin slices prosciutto (about one 3-ounce package)
6 slices (1 ounce each) provolone cheese

1. Spray 12 standard (2¾-inch) muffin cups with nonstick cooking spray. Roll out dough on lightly floured surface to 12×10-inch rectangle.

2. Spread garlic and herb cheese evenly over dough. Arrange prosciutto slices over herb cheese; top with provolone slices. Starting with long side, roll up dough jelly-roll style; pinch seam to seal.

3. Cut crosswise into 1-inch slices; arrange slices cut sides down in prepared muffin cups. Cover; let rise in warm, draft-free place 30 to 40 minutes or until nearly doubled in bulk.

4. Preheat oven to 350°F. Bake rolls about 18 minutes or until golden brown. Loosen edges of rolls with knife; remove from pan to wire rack. Serve warm.

Makes 12 rolls

stromboli

1/4 cup *French's*® Spicy Brown Mustard
2 tablespoons chopped fresh basil *or* 2 teaspoons dried basil leaves
1 tablespoon chopped green olives
1 pound frozen bread dough, thawed at room temperature
1/4 pound sliced salami
1/4 pound sliced provolone cheese
1/4 pound sliced ham
1/8 pound thinly sliced pepperoni (2-inch diameter)
1 egg, beaten
1 teaspoon poppy or sesame seeds

1. Grease baking sheet. Stir mustard, basil and olives in small bowl; set aside.

2. Roll dough on floured surface to 16×10-inch rectangle.* Arrange salami on dough, overlapping slices, leaving 1-inch border around edges. Spread half of the mustard mixture thinly over salami. Arrange provolone and ham over salami. Spread with remaining mustard mixture. Top with pepperoni.

3. Fold one third of dough toward center from long edge of rectangle. Fold second side toward center, enclosing filling. Pinch long edge to seal. Pinch ends together and tuck under dough. Place on prepared baking sheet. Cover; let rise in warm place 15 minutes.

4. Preheat oven to 375°F. Cut shallow crosswise slits 3 inches apart on top of dough. Brush Stromboli lightly with beaten egg; sprinkle with poppy seeds. Bake 25 minutes or until browned. Remove to rack; cool slightly. Serve warm. *Makes 12 servings*

If dough is too hard to roll, allow to rest on floured surface for 5 to 10 minutes.

Pasta, Polenta

and Rice

pasta with fresh tomato-olive sauce

2 tablespoons olive oil
1 small onion, chopped
2 cloves garlic, minced
4 large ripe tomatoes, seeded and chopped (about 3 cups)
$\frac{3}{4}$ teaspoon dried oregano
$\frac{1}{8}$ teaspoon red pepper flakes
$\frac{2}{3}$ cup chopped pitted kalamata olives
1 tablespoon capers (optional)
   Salt and black pepper
1 package (16 ounces) uncooked spaghetti
   Grated Parmesan cheese

1. Heat olive oil in large skillet over medium heat. Add onion and garlic; cook and stir about 4 minutes or until onion is tender.

2. Add tomatoes, oregano and red pepper flakes; simmer, uncovered, 15 to 20 minutes or until sauce is thickened. Stir in olives, capers and salt and pepper to taste.

3. Meanwhile, cook pasta according to package directions; drain. Add pasta to skillet; toss to coat with sauce. Sprinkle with cheese before serving.

Makes 6 to 8 servings

If your skillet is not large enough to hold both the sauce and the cooked spaghetti, toss them together in a heated serving bowl.

polenta squares with chunky tomato sauce

4 cups milk
$\frac{1}{2}$ teaspoon salt
$\frac{1}{4}$ teaspoon ground red pepper
1 cup yellow cornmeal
2 tablespoons butter
$\frac{1}{2}$ cup chopped green bell pepper
$\frac{1}{2}$ cup chopped onion
2 cloves garlic, minced
$\frac{1}{2}$ cup grated Parmesan cheese
1 jar (28 ounces) prepared chunky garden vegetable-style pasta sauce
$1\frac{1}{2}$ cups (6 ounces) shredded provolone cheese

1. Bring milk, salt and red pepper to a boil in large heavy saucepan over medium-high heat. While whisking milk mixture vigorously, add cornmeal in very thin but steady stream (do not let lumps form). Reduce heat to low.

2. Cook, uncovered, 40 to 60 minutes until polenta is very thick, stirring frequently. (Polenta is ready when wooden spoon stands upright in center of mixture.)

3. Meanwhile, melt butter in medium saucepan over medium heat. Add bell pepper, onion and garlic; cook and stir 5 minutes or until vegetables are tender. Remove from saucepan with slotted spoon. Stir bell pepper mixture and Parmesan cheese into polenta.

4. Spray 13×9-inch baking pan with nonstick cooking spray. Spread polenta evenly into baking pan. Cover; let stand at room temperature 6 hours or until completely cooled and firm.

5. Preheat oven to 350°F. Cut polenta into 24 squares. Pour pasta sauce evenly over polenta. Bake 20 to 25 minutes until sauce is bubbly around edges of pan. Remove from oven. Sprinkle with provolone cheese.

6. Bake 2 to 3 minutes just until cheese is melted. Let stand 5 minutes.

Makes 6 to 8 servings

asparagus-parmesan risotto

5$\frac{1}{2}$ cups chicken or vegetable broth
$\frac{1}{8}$ teaspoon salt
 4 tablespoons unsalted butter, divided
$\frac{1}{3}$ cup finely chopped onion
 2 cups uncooked arborio rice
$\frac{2}{3}$ cup dry white wine
2$\frac{1}{2}$ cups fresh asparagus pieces (about 1 inch long)
$\frac{2}{3}$ cup frozen peas
 1 cup grated Parmesan cheese

1. Bring broth and salt to a boil in medium saucepan over medium-high heat; reduce heat to low and simmer.

2. Meanwhile, melt 3 tablespoons butter in large saucepan over medium heat. Add onion; cook and stir 2 to 3 minutes or until tender. Stir in rice; cook 2 minutes or until most of rice grains are opaque, stirring frequently. Add wine; cook, stirring occasionally, until most of wine is absorbed.

3. Add 1$\frac{1}{2}$ cups broth; cook and stir 6 to 7 minutes or until most of liquid is absorbed. (Mixture should simmer, but not boil.) Add 2 cups broth and asparagus; cook and stir 6 to 7 minutes until most of liquid is absorbed. Add remaining 2 cups broth and peas; cook and stir 5 to 6 minutes or until most of liquid is absorbed and rice mixture is creamy.

4. Remove from heat; stir in remaining 1 tablespoon butter and Parmesan cheese until melted. *Makes 4 to 5 main-dish servings*

Asparagus-Spinach Risotto: Substitute 1 cup fresh baby spinach leaves or chopped large spinach leaves for peas. Add spinach at end of step 3; cover and let stand 1 minute or until spinach is wilted. Proceed with step 4.

Asparagus-Chicken Risotto: Add 2 cups chopped or shredded cooked chicken to risotto with peas in step 3. Proceed as directed.

rotini with fresh red & yellow tomato sauce

½ cup (1 stick) **I CAN'T BELIEVE IT'S NOT BUTTER!**® Spread
1 medium onion, chopped
2 cloves garlic, finely chopped (optional)
1½ pounds red and/or yellow cherry tomatoes, halved
⅓ cup chopped fresh basil leaves
1 box (16 ounces) rotini pasta, cooked and drained
Grated Parmesan cheese

In 12-inch nonstick skillet, melt I Can't Believe It's Not Butter!® Spread over medium heat and cook onion, stirring occasionally, 2 minutes or until softened. Stir in garlic and tomatoes and cook, stirring occasionally, 5 minutes or until tomatoes soften but do not lose their shape and sauce thickens slightly. Stir in basil and season, if desired, with salt and ground black pepper.

In large serving bowl, toss sauce with hot rotini and sprinkle with cheese.

Makes 4 servings

Make this dish with any type of pasta. Cook fusilli, linguine or fettucine according to the package directions. Add the fresh tomato and basil sauce for a delightfully light and tasty dish.

gemelli & grilled summer vegetables

2 large bell peppers (red and yellow)
12 stalks asparagus
2 slices red onion
3 tablespoons plus 1 teaspoon olive oil, divided
6 ounces (2$\frac{1}{4}$ cups) uncooked gemelli or rotini pasta
2 tablespoons pine nuts
1 clove garlic
1 cup loosely packed fresh basil leaves
$\frac{1}{4}$ cup grated Parmesan cheese
$\frac{1}{4}$ teaspoon salt
$\frac{1}{4}$ teaspoon black pepper
1 cup grape or cherry tomatoes

1. Prepare grill for direct cooking. Cut bell peppers in half; remove and discard seeds. Grill bell peppers, skin side down, on covered grill over medium heat 10 to 12 minutes or until skins are blackened. Place peppers in paper or plastic bag; let stand 15 minutes. Remove and discard blackened skins. Cut peppers into chunks; place in large bowl.

2. Toss asparagus and onion with 1 teaspoon olive oil. Grill on covered grill over medium heat 8 to 10 minutes or until tender, turning once. Cut asparagus into 2-inch pieces and coarsely chop onion; add asparagus and onion to peppers.

3. Cook pasta according to package directions; drain and add to vegetables.

4. Process pine nuts and garlic in food processor until coarsely chopped. Add basil; process until finely chopped. While processor is running, add remaining 3 tablespoons olive oil. Stir in cheese, salt and pepper. Add basil mixture and tomatoes to pasta and vegetables; toss to coat. Serve immediately. *Makes 4 (1$\frac{1}{2}$-cup) servings*

pesto lasagna

1 package (16 ounces) uncooked lasagna noodles
3 tablespoons olive oil
1½ cups chopped onions
3 cloves garlic, finely chopped
3 packages (10 ounces each) frozen chopped spinach, thawed and squeezed dry
Salt and black pepper
3 cups (24 ounces) ricotta cheese
1½ cups prepared pesto sauce
¾ cup grated Parmesan cheese
½ cup pine nuts, toasted
6 cups (16 ounces) shredded mozzarella cheese
Roasted red pepper strips (optional)

1. Preheat oven to 350°F. Spray 13×9-inch casserole or lasagna pan with nonstick cooking spray. Partially cook lasagna noodles according to package directions.

2. Heat oil in large skillet over medium-high heat. Cook and stir onions and garlic until transparent. Add spinach; cook and stir about 5 minutes. Season with salt and pepper. Transfer to large bowl.

3. Add ricotta cheese, pesto, Parmesan cheese and pine nuts to spinach mixture; mix well.

4. Layer 5 lasagna noodles, slightly overlapping, in prepared pan. Top with one third of ricotta mixture and one third of mozzarella. Repeat layers twice.

5. Bake about 35 minutes or until hot and bubbly. Garnish with roasted red pepper. *Makes 8 servings*

portobello pesto pasta casserole

3 ounces uncooked angel hair pasta, broken into thirds
  Nonstick cooking spray
6 ounces bulk pork sausage
6 ounces sliced portobello mushrooms
2 tablespoons prepared pesto
1 cup packed stemmed spinach (about 2 ounces)
3 tablespoons Italian bread crumbs
1 tablespoon grated Parmesan cheese

1. Preheat broiler. Cook pasta according to package directions.

2. Meanwhile, spray 12-inch nonstick skillet with cooking spray; place over medium heat. Add sausage; cook 4 minutes or until no longer pink, stirring to break up meat. Transfer sausage to plate; set aside.

3. Coat sausage residue remaining in skillet with cooking spray. Add mushrooms to skillet. Coat mushrooms with cooking spray. Cook and stir over medium heat 4 minutes or until mushrooms are tender.

4. Drain pasta. Toss pasta with pesto until evenly coated. Add spinach. Spread evenly over bottom of pie plate. Arrange mushrooms and sausage over top.

5. Mix bread crumbs and cheese in small bowl; sprinkle over casserole. Broil 3 to 4 minutes or until light brown. Remove from oven; let stand 5 minutes before serving.   *Makes 4 servings*

pan-fried polenta
with fresh tomato-bean salsa

2$\frac{1}{2}$ cups chopped plum tomatoes

  1 cup canned white beans, rinsed and drained

$\frac{1}{4}$ cup chopped fresh basil leaves

$\frac{1}{2}$ teaspoon salt

$\frac{1}{2}$ teaspoon black pepper

  2 tablespoons olive oil

  1 package (16 ounces) prepared polenta, sliced into $\frac{1}{4}$-inch-thick rounds

$\frac{1}{4}$ cup grated Parmesan cheese

  Additional basil leaves for garnish

1. Stir together tomatoes, beans, basil, salt and pepper. Let stand at room temperature 15 minutes to blend flavors.

2. Heat 1 tablespoon olive oil in medium nonstick skillet over medium-high heat. Add half of polenta slices to skillet and cook about 4 minutes or until golden brown on both sides, turning once. Remove polenta from skillet. Repeat with remaining oil and polenta slices.

3. Arrange polenta on serving platter. Top with tomato-bean salsa. Sprinkle with cheese and garnish with basil leaves. *Makes 4 servings*

manicotti

1 container (16 ounces) ricotta cheese
2 cups (8 ounces) shredded mozzarella cheese
$\frac{1}{2}$ cup cottage cheese
2 eggs, beaten
2 tablespoons grated Parmesan cheese
$\frac{1}{2}$ teaspoon minced garlic
   Salt and black pepper
1 package (about 8 ounces) uncooked manicotti shells
1 pound ground beef
1 jar (26 ounces) pasta sauce
2 cups water

1. Preheat oven to 375°F.

2. Combine ricotta cheese, mozzarella cheese, cottage cheese, eggs, Parmesan cheese and garlic in large bowl; mix well. Season with salt and pepper. Fill manicotti shells with cheese mixture; place in 13×9-inch baking dish.

3. Brown ground beef in large skillet over medium-high heat, stirring to break up meat. Drain fat. Stir in pasta sauce and water (mixture will be thin). Pour sauce over filled manicotti shells.

4. Cover with foil. Bake 1 hour or until sauce has thickened and shells are tender. *Makes 6 servings*

fettuccine carbonara

1 box (12 ounces) fettuccine noodles
1 cup frozen green peas
1 jar (1 pound) RAGÚ® Cheesy! Light Parmesan Alfredo Sauce
4 slices turkey bacon, crisp-cooked and crumbled

1. Cook fettuccine according to package directions, adding peas during last 2 minutes of cooking; drain and set aside.

2. In 2-quart saucepan, heat Light Parmesan Alfredo Sauce over medium heat; stir in bacon.

3. To serve, toss sauce with hot fettuccine and peas. Sprinkle, if desired, with ground black pepper and grated Parmesan cheese.

Makes 6 servings

ravioli in cream sauce

1 package (about 9 ounces) refrigerated three-cheese ravioli or tortellini
1½ cups frozen peas
1 cup milk
1 package (1¼ ounces) Alfredo or cheese sauce mix
¼ cup (1 ounce) shredded Asiago cheese
¼ teaspoon nutmeg (optional)

1. Add ravioli and peas to large saucepan of salted boiling water. Cook over high heat 5 minutes or until ravioli are tender. Drain; return ravioli mixture to pan.

2. Add milk and Alfredo mix. Bring to a boil. Reduce heat to medium. Cook 2 minutes or until sauce is thickened. Sprinkle with cheese and nutmeg.

Makes 4 servings

pasta with creamy vodka sauce

6 ounces uncooked campanelle or bowtie pasta
3 plum tomatoes, seeded and chopped
2 cloves garlic, minced
1 tablespoon unsalted butter
3 tablespoons vodka
$\frac{1}{2}$ cup whipping cream
$\frac{1}{4}$ teaspoon salt
$\frac{1}{4}$ teaspoon red pepper flakes
$\frac{1}{3}$ cup grated Parmesan cheese
2 tablespoons snipped chives

1. Cook pasta according to package directions; drain. Keep warm in pan.

2. Melt butter in large skillet over medium heat. Add tomatoes and garlic; cook 3 minutes, stirring frequently. Add vodka; simmer about 2 minutes or until most liquid has evaporated.

3. Stir in cream, salt and red pepper flakes; return to a simmer. Simmer 2 to 3 minutes or until slightly thickened. Remove from heat; let stand 2 minutes. Stir in cheese until melted.

4. Add sauce and chives to pasta; toss until pasta is coated. Serve immediately. *Makes 4 to 5 servings*

polenta with pasta sauce & vegetables

1 can (about 14 ounces) chicken and vegetable broth

1½ cups water

1 cup yellow cornmeal

2 teaspoons olive oil

12 ounces assorted cut-up vegetables, such as broccoli florets, bell peppers, red onions, zucchini squash and thin carrot strips

2 teaspoons minced garlic

2 cups prepared tomato-basil pasta sauce

½ cup grated Asiago cheese

¼ cup chopped fresh basil (optional)

1. To prepare polenta, whisk together chicken broth, water and cornmeal in large microwavable bowl. Cover with waxed paper; microwave on HIGH 5 minutes. Whisk well and microwave on HIGH 4 to 5 minutes more or until polenta is very thick. Whisk again; cover and keep warm.

2. Meanwhile, heat oil in large, deep nonstick skillet over medium heat. Add vegetables and garlic; cook and stir 5 minutes. Add pasta sauce; reduce heat, cover and simmer 5 to 8 minutes or until vegetables are tender.

3. Spoon polenta onto serving plates; top with pasta sauce mixture. Sprinkle with cheese and basil.

Makes 4 servings

baked gnocchi

1 package (about 17 ounces) gnocchi (frozen or vacuum-packed)
⅓ cup olive oil
3 cloves garlic, minced
1 package (10 ounces) frozen spinach, thawed and squeezed dry
1 can (about 14 ounces) diced tomatoes
1 teaspoon Italian seasoning
   Salt and black pepper
½ cup grated Parmesan cheese
½ cup (2 ounces) shredded mozzarella cheese

1. Preheat oven to 350°F. Grease large casserole or gratin dish. Cook gnocchi according to package directions. Drain and set aside.

2. Heat oil in large skillet or Dutch oven over medium heat. Add garlic; cook and stir 30 seconds. Stir in spinach. Cook, covered, 2 minutes or until spinach wilts. Add tomatoes and Italian seasoning. Season with salt and pepper; cook and stir about 5 minutes. Add gnocchi to spinach mixture in skillet; stir gently.

3. Transfer gnocchi mixture to prepared dish. Sprinkle with Parmesan and mozzarella cheeses. Bake 20 to 30 minutes or until casserole is bubbly and cheese is melted.   *Makes 4 to 6 servings*

quick pasta with peppers

8 ounces uncooked penne or rigatoni pasta
2 tablespoons olive oil
1 each red, yellow and green bell pepper, thinly sliced
1 jar (26 ounces) marinara sauce
$\frac{1}{4}$ cup grated Parmesan cheese

1. Cook pasta according to package directions; drain and keep warm.

2. Meanwhile, heat oil in large skillet over medium-high heat. Add bell peppers; cook 2 minutes, stirring frequently. Reduce heat to medium-low; stir in sauce. Cook and stir 5 minutes over medium heat, stirring frequently.

3. Pour sauce over hot pasta; sprinkle with cheese before serving.

Makes 6 to 8 servings

Variation: Add 1 cup coarsely chopped pepperoni with the pasta sauce.

tuscan-style fettuccine with artichokes

$\frac{1}{2}$ cup (1 stick) **I CAN'T BELIEVE IT'S NOT BUTTER!**® Spread
1 can (14 ounces) artichoke hearts, drained and chopped
$\frac{1}{3}$ cup chopped fresh cilantro (optional)
2 tablespoons chopped fresh oregano leaves *or* 1 teaspoon
   dried oregano leaves, crushed
2 tablespoons finely chopped garlic
$\frac{1}{2}$ teaspoon ground black pepper
1 box (16 ounces) fettuccine, cooked and drained
   Grated Parmesan cheese

In 12-inch skillet, melt I Can't Believe It's Not Butter!® Spread over medium-high heat and cook artichokes, cilantro, oregano, garlic and pepper, stirring occasionally, 3 minutes or until heated through. To serve, toss sauce with hot fettuccine and sprinkle with cheese. *Makes 6 servings*

classic fettuccine alfredo

12 ounces uncooked fettuccine
$^2/_3$ cup whipping cream
 6 tablespoons unsalted butter
$^1/_2$ teaspoon salt
   Generous dash white pepper
   Generous dash ground nutmeg
 1 cup grated Parmesan cheese
 2 tablespoons chopped fresh parsley

1. Cook pasta according to package directions; drain well and keep warm in pan.

2. Meanwhile, heat cream and butter in large heavy skillet over medium-low heat until butter melts and mixture bubbles, stirring frequently. Cook and stir 2 minutes. Stir in salt, white pepper and nutmeg. Remove from heat. Gradually stir in cheese until well blended and smooth. Return to heat briefly to completely blend cheese, if necessary. (Do not let sauce bubble or cheese will become lumpy and tough.)

3. Pour sauce over pasta. Toss with two forks over low heat 2 to 3 minutes or until sauce is thickened and pasta is evenly coated. Sprinkle with chopped parsley. Serve immediately   *Makes 4 servings*

tuscan baked rigatoni

1 pound Italian sausage, casings removed
1 package (16 ounces) rigatoni, cooked, drained and kept warm
2 cups (8 ounces) shredded fontina cheese
2 tablespoons olive oil
2 bulbs fennel, thinly sliced
4 cloves garlic, minced
1 can (28 ounces) crushed tomatoes
1 cup whipping cream
1 teaspoon salt
1 teaspoon black pepper
8 cups packed torn stemmed spinach
1 can (about 15 ounces) cannellini beans, rinsed and drained
2 tablespoons pine nuts
$\frac{1}{2}$ cup grated Parmesan cheese

1. Preheat oven to 350°F. Coat 4-quart casserole with nonstick cooking spray; set aside.

2. Brown sausage in large skillet over medium-high heat, stirring to break up meat. Drain fat. Transfer sausage to large bowl. Add rigatoni and fontina cheese; mix well.

3. Heat oil in same skillet; add fennel and garlic. Cook and stir over medium heat 3 minutes or until fennel is tender. Add tomatoes, cream, salt and pepper; cook and stir until slightly thickened. Stir in spinach, beans and pine nuts; cook until heated through.

4. Pour sauce mixture over pasta mixture; toss to coat. Transfer to prepared casserole; sprinkle evenly with Parmesan cheese. Bake 30 minutes or until bubbly and heated through.   *Makes 6 to 8 servings*

mushroom ragoût with polenta

1 package (about $\frac{1}{2}$ ounce) dried porcini mushrooms

$\frac{1}{2}$ cup boiling water

1 can (about 14 ounces) vegetable broth

$\frac{1}{2}$ cup yellow cornmeal

1 tablespoon olive oil

$\frac{1}{3}$ cup sliced shallots or chopped onion

1 package (4 ounces) sliced mixed fresh exotic mushrooms or sliced
    cremini (brown) mushrooms

4 cloves garlic, minced

1 can (about 14 ounces) Italian-style diced tomatoes

$\frac{1}{4}$ teaspoon red pepper flakes

$\frac{1}{4}$ cup chopped fresh basil or parsley

$\frac{1}{2}$ cup grated Parmesan cheese

1. Soak porcini mushrooms in boiling water 10 minutes.

2. Meanwhile, whisk together vegetable broth and cornmeal in large microwavable bowl. Cover with waxed paper; microwave on HIGH 5 minutes. Whisk well; cook on HIGH 3 to 4 minutes or until polenta is very thick. Whisk again; cover. Set aside.

3. Heat oil in large nonstick skillet over medium-high heat. Add shallots; cook and stir 3 minutes. Add fresh mushrooms and garlic; cook and stir 3 to 4 minutes. Add tomatoes and red pepper flakes.

4. Drain porcini mushrooms, reserving liquid. Strain liquid and add to skillet. If mushrooms are large, cut into $\frac{1}{2}$-inch pieces; add to skillet. Bring to a boil over high heat. Reduce heat; simmer, uncovered, 5 minutes or until slightly thickened. Stir in basil.

5. Spoon polenta onto 4 plates; top with mushroom mixture. Sprinkle with cheese.   *Makes 4 servings*

baked pasta with ricotta

1 package (16 ounces) uncooked rigatoni or penne pasta
1 container (15 ounces) ricotta cheese
$\frac{2}{3}$ cup grated Parmesan cheese
2 eggs, lightly beaten
$\frac{1}{2}$ teaspoon salt
$\frac{1}{8}$ teaspoon black pepper
2 jars (26 ounces each) marinara sauce, divided
3 cups (12 ounces) shredded mozzarella cheese, divided

1. Preheat oven to 375°F. Spray 13×9-inch baking pan with nonstick cooking spray.

2. Cook rigatoni according to package directions; drain. Meanwhile, beat ricotta, Parmesan, eggs, salt and pepper in medium bowl until well blended.

3. Spread 2 cups marinara sauce over bottom of prepared pan; spoon half of cooked pasta over sauce. Top with half of ricotta mixture and 1 cup mozzarella. Repeat layers of marinara sauce, pasta and ricotta mixture. Top with 1 cup mozzarella, remaining marinara sauce and 1 cup mozzarella.

4. Cover with foil. Bake about 1 hour or until bubbly. Uncover and bake about 5 minutes more or until cheese is completely melted. Let stand 15 minutes before serving   *Makes 12 servings*

Pasta, Polenta and Rice

veggie no boiling lasagna

1 tablespoon olive oil
1 medium sweet onion, thinly sliced
1 medium red bell pepper, thinly sliced
1 medium zucchini, cut in half lengthwise and thinly sliced
2 containers (15 ounces each) ricotta cheese
2 cups shredded mozzarella cheese (about 8 ounces), divided
$\frac{1}{2}$ cup grated Parmesan cheese, divided
2 eggs
2 jars (1 pound 10 ounces each) RAGÚ® Old World Style® Pasta Sauce
12 uncooked lasagna noodles

1. Preheat oven to 375°F. In 12-inch nonstick skillet, heat olive oil over medium-high heat and cook onion, red bell pepper and zucchini, stirring occasionally, 5 minutes or until softened.

2. Meanwhile, combine ricotta cheese, 1 cup mozzarella cheese, $\frac{1}{4}$ cup Parmesan cheese and eggs.

3. In 13×9-inch baking dish, spread 1 cup Pasta Sauce. Layer 4 uncooked noodles, then 1 cup Sauce, half of ricotta mixture and half of vegetables; repeat. Top with remaining uncooked noodles and 2 cups Sauce. Reserve remaining Sauce.

4. Cover with foil and bake 1 hour. Remove foil; sprinkle with remaining cheeses. Bake uncovered 10 minutes. Let stand 10 minutes before serving. Serve with reserved Pasta Sauce, heated.   *Makes 12 servings*

fettuccine gorgonzola
with sun-dried tomatoes

4 ounces sun-dried tomatoes (not packed in oil)
8 ounces uncooked spinach or tricolor fettuccine
1 cup cottage cheese
½ cup plain yogurt
½ cup (2 ounces) crumbled Gorgonzola cheese, plus
  additional for garnish
⅛ teaspoon white pepper

1. Place sun-dried tomatoes in small bowl; pour hot water over to cover. Let stand 15 minutes or until tomatoes are soft. Drain well; cut into strips. Cook pasta according to package directions, omitting salt. Drain well. Cover and keep warm.

2. Meanwhile, process cottage cheese and yogurt in food processor or blender until smooth. Heat cottage cheese mixture in large skillet over low heat. Add Gorgonzola cheese and white pepper; stir until cheese is melted.

3. Add pasta and tomatoes to skillet; toss to coat with sauce. Garnish with additional Gorgonzola cheese. Serve immediately. *Makes 4 servings*

ravioli with tomato pesto

4 ounces frozen cheese ravioli
1¼ cups coarsely chopped plum tomatoes
¼ cup fresh basil leaves
2 teaspoons pine nuts
2 teaspoons olive oil
¼ teaspoon salt
⅛ teaspoon black pepper
1 tablespoon grated Parmesan cheese

1. Cook ravioli according to package directions; drain.

2. Meanwhile, combine tomatoes, basil, pine nuts, oil, salt and pepper in food processor. Process using on/off pulses just until ingredients are chopped. Serve sauce over hot cooked ravioli. Top with cheese.

Makes 2 servings

Ravioli are stuffed pasta with various mixtures such as cheese, meat or vegetables. Although homemade ravioli are fabulous, the prepared varieties found in the refrigerated or freezer sections of the supermarket are one of the best convenience foods available. Just prepare as directed and top with your favorite sauce.

tuscan pasta

12 ounces uncooked rigatoni or any shaped pasta
Tuscan Tomato Sauce (recipe follows)
$\frac{1}{3}$ cup grated Parmesan cheese, or to taste

1. Cook pasta according to package directions until al dente; drain.

2. Serve sauce over pasta. Serve with cheese. *Makes 6 servings*

tuscan tomato sauce

2 tablespoons olive oil
$\frac{1}{2}$ cup chopped onion
2 cloves garlic, minced
8 plum tomatoes, coarsely chopped
1 can (8 ounces) tomato sauce
1 teaspoon *each* chopped fresh basil, oregano and rosemary
$\frac{1}{2}$ teaspoon salt
$\frac{1}{2}$ teaspoon black pepper

1. Heat oil in medium nonstick saucepan over medium heat. Add onion; cook and stir about 4 minutes or until tender. Add garlic; cook 1 minute.

2. Stir in tomatoes, tomato sauce, herbs, salt and pepper; bring to a boil. Reduce heat and simmer, uncovered, about 6 minutes or until desired consistency is reached, stirring occasionally. *Makes 3 cups*

Pasta, Polenta and Rice

Meat and Poultry

braciola

1 can (28 ounces) tomato sauce
2$\frac{1}{2}$ teaspoons dried oregano, divided
1$\frac{1}{4}$ teaspoons dried basil, divided
1 teaspoon salt
$\frac{1}{2}$ pound bulk hot Italian sausage or hot Italian sausage links, casings removed
$\frac{1}{2}$ cup chopped onion
$\frac{1}{4}$ cup grated Parmesan cheese
2 cloves garlic, minced
1 tablespoon dried parsley flakes
1 to 2 beef flank steaks (about 2$\frac{1}{2}$ pounds)

Slow Cooker Directions

1. Combine tomato sauce, 2 teaspoons oregano, 1 teaspoon basil and salt in medium bowl; set aside.

2. Brown sausage in large nonstick skillet over medium-high heat, stirring to break up meat. Drain fat. Combine sausage, onion, cheese, garlic, parsley, remaining $\frac{1}{2}$ teaspoon oregano and remaining $\frac{1}{4}$ teaspoon basil in medium bowl; set aside.

3. Place steak between pieces of waxed paper. Pound with meat mallet until steak is $\frac{1}{4}$ inch thick. Cut steak into 3-inch-wide strips.

4. Spoon sausage mixture evenly onto each steak strip. Roll up, jelly-roll style, securing meat with toothpicks. Place each roll in slow cooker. Pour reserved tomato sauce mixture over rolls. Cover; cook on LOW 6 to 8 hours or until beef is tender.

5. Cut each roll into slices. Top with hot tomato sauce.

Makes 8 servings

gremolata pasta skillet

2 tablespoons olive oil

3 cloves garlic, minced

1 package (9 ounces) grilled chicken breast strips

2 cups chicken broth

2 tablespoons lemon juice

2 cups uncooked farfalle (bowtie) pasta

$\frac{1}{4}$ cup chopped fresh Italian parsley

$\frac{1}{4}$ cup shredded Parmesan cheese

1 tablespoon grated lemon peel

Black pepper

Additional shredded Parmesan cheese (optional)

1. Heat oil in large nonstick skillet over medium high heat. Add garlic; cook 2 to 3 minutes or until soft. Add chicken, broth and lemon juice; bring to a boil.

2. Stir in pasta; reduce heat to medium low. Cover; cook 10 minutes.

3. Stir in parsley, Parmesan and lemon peel. Sprinkle with black pepper and additional cheese. *Makes about 4 (1-cup) servings*

Variation: Add 2 cups fresh broccoli flowerets or chopped asparagus with the pasta.

chicken piccata

3 tablespoons all-purpose flour
$\frac{1}{2}$ teaspoon salt
$\frac{1}{4}$ teaspoon black pepper
4 boneless skinless chicken breasts (4 ounces each)
2 teaspoons olive oil
1 teaspoon butter
2 cloves garlic, minced
$\frac{3}{4}$ cup chicken broth
1 tablespoon fresh lemon juice
2 tablespoons chopped fresh Italian parsley
1 tablespoon drained capers

1. Combine flour, salt and pepper in shallow dish. Reserve 1 tablespoon flour mixture.

2. Place chicken between sheets of plastic wrap. Using flat side of meat mallet or rolling pin, pound chicken to $\frac{1}{2}$-inch thickness. Coat chicken in flour mixture, shaking off excess.

3. Heat oil and butter in large nonstick skillet over medium heat until butter is melted. Cook chicken 4 to 5 minutes per side or until no longer pink in center. Transfer to serving platter; cover loosely with foil.

4. Add garlic to same skillet; cook and stir over medium heat 1 minute. Add reserved flour mixture; cook and stir 1 minute. Add broth and lemon juice; cook 2 minutes, stirring frequently, until sauce thickens. Stir in parsley and capers; spoon sauce over chicken. *Makes 4 servings*

Meat and Poultry

osso bucco

1 large onion, cut into thin wedges
2 large carrots, sliced
4 cloves garlic, sliced
4 veal shanks (3 to 4 pounds)
2 teaspoons herbes de Provence*
1 teaspoon salt
$\frac{1}{2}$ teaspoon black pepper
$\frac{3}{4}$ cup beef consommé or beef broth
$\frac{1}{4}$ cup dry vermouth (optional)
3 tablespoons flour
3 tablespoons water
$\frac{1}{4}$ cup minced parsley
1 small clove garlic, minced
1 teaspoon grated lemon peel

*Or substitute $\frac{1}{2}$ teaspoon each dried thyme, rosemary, oregano and basil.

Slow Cooker Directions

1. Coat slow cooker with cooking spray. Place onion, carrots and sliced garlic in bottom of slow cooker. Arrange veal over vegetables, overlapping slightly. Sprinkle with herbs, salt and pepper. Add broth and vermouth, if desired.

2. Cover; cook 8 to 9 hours on LOW or 5 to 6 hours on HIGH or until veal and vegetables are tender.

3. Transfer veal and vegetables to serving platter. Cover with foil; keep warm. Turn slow cooker to HIGH. Mix flour with water until smooth. Stir into slow cooker. Cook 15 minutes or until sauce thickens.

4. Serve sauce over veal and vegetables. Combine parsley, minced garlic and lemon peel; sprinkle over veal and vegetables.   *Makes 4 servings*

italian sausage and peppers

3 cups red, yellow and green bell pepper chunks (1-inch)*
1 small onion, cut into thin wedges
3 cloves garlic, minced
4 links hot or mild Italian sausage (about 1 pound)
1 cup pasta or marinara sauce
$1/4$ cup red wine or port
1 tablespoon cornstarch
1 tablespoon water
   Hot cooked spaghetti
$1/4$ cup grated Parmesan or Romano cheese

*Look for mixed bell pepper chunks at the supermarket salad bar.

Slow Cooker Directions

1. Coat slow cooker with cooking spray. Place bell peppers, onion and garlic in slow cooker. Arrange sausage over vegetables. Combine pasta sauce and wine; pour over sausage. Cover; cook on LOW 8 to 9 hours or on HIGH 4 to 5 hours.

2. Transfer sausage to serving platter. Cover with foil; keep warm. Let liquid in slow cooker stand 5 minutes to allow fat to rise. Skim off fat.

3. Turn heat to HIGH. Mix cornstarch with water until smooth; stir into slow cooker. Cook 15 minutes or until sauce is thickened, stirring once. Serve sauce with spaghetti and sausage; top with cheese.   *Makes 4 servings*

cacciatore chicken melt

4 boneless skinless chicken thighs or breasts
1 tablespoon oil
1 teaspoon minced garlic in olive oil
1 jar (28 ounces) mushroom pasta sauce
1 cup shredded mozzarella cheese
4 large slices crusty Italian bread, lightly toasted

1. Cut chicken thighs in half horizontally to make cutlets. Heat oil in large skillet over medium-high heat. Add chicken and garlic; brown 3 minutes per side. Stir in pasta sauce. Cover; cook over medium heat 15 minutes or chicken is cooked through.

2. Divide cheese evenly over chicken. Cover; cook 1 minute or until cheese is melted slightly. Top each slice of toast with 2 chicken cutlets. Evenly divide sauce over chicken.

Makes 4 servings

Cacciatore (cacciatora, alla) refers to dishes prepared "hunter style." Chicken Cacciatore is a popular dish in which the chicken pieces are prepared in a spicy tomato sauce with mushrooms and herbs.

saltimbocca

4 boneless thin veal slices cut from the leg, or thinly sliced
veal cutlets (about 1¼ pounds)
1 tablespoon FILIPPO BERIO® Olive Oil
1 clove garlic, cut in half
4 slices prosciutto, cut into halves
8 fresh sage leaves*
½ cup beef broth
5 tablespoons Marsala wine or medium sherry
¼ cup half-and-half
Freshly ground black pepper

*Omit sage if fresh is unavailable. Do not substitute dried sage leaves.

Pound veal between 2 pieces waxed paper with flat side of meat mallet
or rolling pin until very thin. Cut each piece in half to make 8 small pieces.
In large skillet, heat olive oil with garlic over medium heat until hot. Add
veal; cook until brown, turning occasionally. Top each piece with slice of
prosciutto and sage leaf. Add beef broth and Marsala. Cover; reduce heat
to low and simmer 5 minutes or until veal is cooked through and tender.
Transfer veal to warm serving platter; keep warm. Add half-and-half to
mixture in skillet; simmer 5 to 8 minutes, stirring occasionally, until liquid is
reduced and thickened, scraping bottom of skillet to loosen browned bits.
Remove garlic. Spoon sauce over veal. Season to taste with pepper.

Makes 4 servings

baked italian meatballs

1 pound ground beef (90% to 95% lean)
$^1/_4$ cup seasoned dry bread crumbs
1 egg
2 tablespoons water
1 teaspoon minced garlic
$^1/_2$ teaspoon salt
$^1/_8$ teaspoon black pepper
1 jar (14$^1/_2$ ounces) pasta sauce, heated
Hot cooked pasta or crusty Italian rolls (optional)

1. Heat oven to 400°F. Combine ground beef, bread crumbs, egg, water, garlic, salt and pepper in large bowl, mixing lightly but thoroughly. Shape into 12 two-inch meatballs. Place on rack in broiler pan. Bake in 400°F oven 17 to 19 minutes to medium (160°F) doneness, until not pink in center and juices show no pink color.

2. Serve with pasta sauce over hot cooked pasta or as sandwiches in crusty Italian rolls, if desired. *Makes 4 servings*

Favorite recipe from **National Cattlemen's Beef Association** on behalf of The Beef Checkoff

chicken florentine

4 skinless, boneless chicken breast halves (6 ounces each)
$\frac{1}{4}$ teaspoon salt
$\frac{1}{4}$ teaspoon freshly ground black pepper
$\frac{1}{2}$ cup Italian seasoned dry bread crumbs
1 egg, separated
1 package (10 ounces) frozen chopped spinach, thawed, well drained
$\frac{1}{8}$ teaspoon nutmeg
2 tablespoons olive oil
4 slices SARGENTO® Deli Style Sliced Mozzarella Cheese
1 cup prepared tomato-basil or marinara pasta sauce, heated

1. Sprinkle chicken with salt and pepper. Place bread crumbs in a shallow plate. Beat egg white in a shallow bowl. Dip each chicken breast in egg white, letting excess drip off, roll lightly in crumbs, patting to coat well. (At this point, chicken may be covered and refrigerated up to 4 hours before cooking.)

2. Combine spinach, egg yolk and nutmeg; mix well. Heat oil in a large skillet over medium-high heat until hot. Add chicken breasts; cook 3 minutes per side or until golden brown. Reduce heat to low. Top each chicken breast with $\frac{1}{4}$ of spinach mixture and 1 slice of cheese. Cover skillet and continue cooking 6 minutes or until chicken is no longer pink in center. Serve with pasta sauce.　　　　*Makes 4 servings*

tuscan chicken with white beans

1 large bulb fennel (about ³⁄₄ pound)
1 teaspoon olive oil
1 teaspoon dried rosemary
¹⁄₂ teaspoon black pepper
¹⁄₂ pound boneless skinless chicken thighs, cut into ³⁄₄-inch pieces
1 can (about 14 ounces) stewed tomatoes
1 can (about 14 ounces) chicken broth
1 can (about 15 ounces) cannellini beans, rinsed and drained
   Hot pepper sauce (optional)

1. Chop and reserve ¼ cup green leafy fennel tops. Chop bulb into ½-inch pieces. Heat oil in large saucepan over medium heat. Add chopped fennel bulb; cook 5 minutes, stirring occasionally.

2. Sprinkle rosemary and pepper over chicken; add to saucepan. Cook and stir 2 minutes. Add tomatoes and broth; bring to a boil. Cover; simmer 10 minutes.

3. Stir in beans; simmer, uncovered, 15 minutes or until chicken is cooked through and sauce thickens. Season to taste with hot pepper sauce. Ladle into 4 shallow bowls; top with reserved fennel tops.   *Makes 4 servings*

italian-style pot roast

2 teaspoons minced garlic
1 teaspoon salt
1 teaspoon dried basil
1 teaspoon dried oregano
$^{1}/_{4}$ teaspoon red pepper flakes
1 boneless beef bottom round rump or chuck shoulder roast
(about $2^{1}/_{2}$ to 3 pounds)
1 large onion, quartered and thinly sliced
$1^{1}/_{2}$ cups tomato-basil or marinara pasta sauce
2 cans (about 15 ounces each) cannellini or Great Northern beans,
rinsed and drained
$^{1}/_{4}$ cup shredded fresh basil or chopped Italian parsley

Slow Cooker Directions

1. Combine garlic, salt, dried basil, oregano and pepper flakes in small bowl; rub over roast.

2. Place half of onion slices in 4-quart slow cooker. Cut roast in half. Place one half of roast over onion slices; top with remaining onion slices and other half of roast. Pour pasta sauce over roast. Cover; cook on LOW 8 to 9 hours or until roast is fork tender.

3. Remove roast to cutting board; tent with foil. Let liquid in slow cooker stand 5 minutes to allow fat to rise. Skim off fat.

4. Stir beans into liquid. Cover; cook on HIGH 15 to 30 minutes or until beans are hot. Carve roast across the grain into thin slices. Serve with bean mixture and fresh basil. *Makes 6 to 8 servings*

chicken cacciatore

8 ounces uncooked pasta
1 can (about 14 ounces) chunky Italian-style tomato sauce
1 cup sliced onion
1 cup sliced mushrooms
1 cup chopped green bell pepper
  Nonstick cooking spray
4 boneless skinless chicken breasts (about 1 pound)
  Salt and black pepper

1. Cook pasta according to package directions; drain and keep warm.

2. While pasta is cooking, combine tomato sauce, onion, mushrooms and bell pepper in microwavable dish. Cover loosely with plastic wrap or waxed paper; microwave on HIGH 6 to 8 minutes, stirring halfway through cooking time.

3. Meanwhile, coat large skillet with cooking spray; heat over medium-high heat. Cook chicken breasts 3 to 4 minutes per side or until lightly browned.

4. Add sauce mixture to skillet; season with salt and pepper. Reduce heat to medium; simmer 12 to 15 minutes. Serve over pasta.

Makes 4 servings

handkerchief pasta with chicken and chard

2 bunches chard
1 package (about 8 ounces) flat lasagna noodles
4 tablespoons extra-virgin olive oil, divided
3 cloves garlic, minced
2 boneless skinless chicken breasts, cut into bite-size pieces
$\frac{1}{4}$ cup balsamic vinegar
   Salt and black pepper
   Toasted pine nuts

1. Trim chard; pull leaves from large stems. Chop stems; roll leaves into bundles and slice into ribbons. Measure 9 loosely packed cups. Set aside.

2. Bring large saucepan of salted water to a boil. Break lasagna noodles into halves or thirds to made square pasta. (Don't worry if some pieces break unevenly.) Cook pasta in boiling water until tender but firm. Drain; oil lightly to prevent sticking. Keep warm.

3. Heat 2 tablespoons oil in large skillet or Dutch oven over medium heat. Add garlic; cook and stir 30 seconds. Add chicken; cook and stir about 2 minutes. Add remaining 2 tablespoons oil; mix in chard. Cover and cook until chard is wilted, stirring occasionally. Stir in vinegar. Cook 3 to 5 minutes or until chicken is cooked through. Season with salt and pepper.

4. Arrange 3 or 4 pieces of pasta on each serving plate; top with chicken mixture. Sprinkle with pine nuts. *Makes 4 servings*

chicken tetrazzini

8 ounces uncooked spaghetti, broken in half
3 tablespoons butter, divided
$\frac{1}{4}$ cup all-purpose flour
1 teaspoon salt
$\frac{1}{2}$ teaspoon paprika
$\frac{1}{2}$ teaspoon celery salt
$\frac{1}{8}$ teaspoon pepper
2 cups milk
1 cup chicken broth
3 cups chopped cooked chicken
1 can (4 ounces) mushrooms, drained
$\frac{1}{4}$ cup pimiento strips
$\frac{3}{4}$ cup (3 ounces) grated Wisconsin Parmesan cheese, divided

In large saucepan, cook spaghetti according to package directions; drain.
Return to same saucepan; add 1 tablespoon butter. Stir until melted. Set
aside. In 3-quart saucepan, melt remaining 2 tablespoons butter over
medium heat; stir in flour, salt, paprika, celery salt and pepper. Remove
from heat; gradually stir in milk and chicken broth. Cook over medium heat,
stirring constantly, until thickened. Add chicken, mushrooms, pimiento,
spaghetti and $\frac{1}{4}$ cup cheese; heat thoroughly. Place chicken mixture on
ovenproof platter or in shallow casserole; sprinkle remaining $\frac{1}{2}$ cup cheese
over top. Broil about 3 inches from heat until lightly browned.

Makes 6 to 8 servings

Favorite recipe from **Wisconsin Milk Marketing Board**

Meat and Poultry

beef spiedini with orzo

¼ cup olive oil
¼ cup dry red wine
2 cloves garlic, minced
1 teaspoon dried rosemary
½ teaspoon coarse salt
½ teaspoon dried thyme
½ teaspoon coarsely ground black pepper
1½ pounds beef top sirloin steak, cut into 1×1¼-inch pieces
1 cup uncooked orzo
6 cups water
½ teaspoon salt
1 tablespoon butter
1 tablespoon chopped parsley
Fresh rosemary sprigs (optional)

1. Combine oil, wine, garlic, dried rosemary, coarse salt, thyme and pepper in large food storage bag. Add beef; turn to coat. Marinate 15 to 30 minutes.

2. Prepare grill for direct cooking. Soak eight 6- to 8-inch bamboo skewers in water 15 minutes.

3. Place water and salt in small pan; bring to a boil. Add orzo; reduce heat and simmer 15 minutes or until tender. Drain. Stir in butter and parsley; keep warm.

4. Thread beef onto skewers. Grill over medium-high heat 8 to 10 minutes, turning occasionally. Garnish skewers with fresh rosemary. Serve with orzo.

Makes 4 servings

fusilli pizzaiola with turkey meatballs

1 pound ground turkey
1 egg, lightly beaten
1 tablespoon milk
$\frac{1}{4}$ cup Italian-seasoned dry bread crumbs
2 tablespoons chopped fresh parsley
$\frac{1}{4}$ teaspoon black pepper, divided
$\frac{1}{2}$ cup chopped onion
$\frac{1}{2}$ cup grated carrots
1 clove garlic, minced
2 teaspoons olive oil
2 cans (about 14 ounces each) diced tomatoes
2 tablespoons chopped fresh basil *or* 2 teaspoons dried basil
1 tablespoon tomato paste
$\frac{1}{2}$ teaspoon dried thyme
1 bay leaf
8 ounces uncooked fusilli or other spiral-shaped pasta

1. Preheat oven to 350°F. Combine turkey, egg and milk in medium bowl. Add bread crumbs, parsley and $\frac{1}{8}$ teaspoon black pepper; mix well. With wet hands, shape turkey mixture into 24 (1-inch) meatballs. Spray baking sheet with nonstick cooking spray. Arrange meatballs on baking sheet. Bake 25 minutes or until no longer pink in center.

2. Place onion, carrots, garlic and oil in medium saucepan. Cook and stir over high heat 5 minutes or until onion is tender. Add tomatoes, basil, tomato paste, thyme, bay leaf and remaining $\frac{1}{8}$ teaspoon black pepper. Bring to a boil; reduce heat to low. Simmer 25 minutes; add meatballs. Cover; simmer 5 to 10 minutes or until sauce thickens slightly. Remove and discard bay leaf.

3. Meanwhile, cook pasta according to package directions. Drain well. Place in large serving bowl. Spoon meatballs and sauce over pasta.

Makes 4 servings

white bean and chicken ragout

2 boneless skinless chicken thighs
2 carrots, cut into $1/2$-inch pieces
2 celery stalks, cut into $1/2$-inch pieces
$1/4$ medium onion, chopped
1 clove garlic
1 bay leaf
1 sprig fresh parsley
1 sprig fresh thyme
3 black peppercorns
1 cup cooked cannellini beans
1 plum tomato, chopped
1 teaspoon herbes de Provence
$1/2$ teaspoon salt
$1/8$ teaspoon black pepper
1 teaspoon extra-virgin olive oil
1 tablespoon chopped fresh parsley
Grated peel of 1 lemon

1. Place chicken thighs in medium saucepan; add cool water to cover. Add carrots, celery, onion, garlic, bay leaf, parsley, thyme and peppercorns. Bring to a boil; reduce heat to low. Simmer 15 to 20 minutes or until tender.

2. Remove chicken from saucepan; let cool 5 minutes.

3. Drain vegetables; reserve broth. Discard garlic, bay leaf, parsley, thyme and peppercorns. Return vegetables to saucepan.

4. Cut chicken into bite-size pieces; add to saucepan with vegetables. Stir in beans, tomato, herbes de Provence, salt and pepper. Add 1 cup broth; simmer 5 minutes.

5. Divide between 2 bowls; drizzle with olive oil. Sprinkle with chopped parsley and lemon peel. *Makes 2 servings*

tuscan beef

1 tablespoon olive oil
2 cloves garlic, minced
1½ teaspoons dried rosemary, divided
1 teaspoon salt
½ teaspoon black pepper
4 boneless beef rib eye or strip steaks (8 to 10 ounces each),
cut ¾ to 1 inch thick
¾ cup prepared tomato-basil or marinara pasta sauce
½ cup sliced pimiento-stuffed green olives
1 tablespoon drained capers

1. Prepare grill for direct cooking or preheat broiler. Combine oil, garlic, 1 teaspoon rosemary, salt and pepper in small bowl; mix well. Spread mixture evenly over both sides of steaks.

2. Grill steaks, covered, over medium-hot coals or broil 4 inches from heat 4 to 5 minutes per side for medium-rare (145°F internal temperature) or to desired doneness.

3. Meanwhile, combine pasta sauce, olives, capers and remaining ½ teaspoon rosemary in small saucepan; mix well. Heat until hot but not boiling. Transfer steaks to serving plates; top with sauce.

Makes 4 servings

Note: Prepared pasta sauces contain a very wide range of sodium. Since olives and capers both add salt, choose a pasta sauce with less sodium for the best results.

Meat and Poultry

chicken prosciutto rolls

1 can (28 ounces) tomato sauce
2 cloves garlic, minced
1 teaspoon dried oregano
1 teaspoon dried basil
4 boneless skinless chicken breasts
8 slices prosciutto
1 jar (12 ounces) roasted red peppers, drained and halved
1 cup grated Asiago cheese, divided
  Hot cooked spaghetti

1. Preheat oven to 350°F. Combine tomato sauce, garlic, oregano and basil in medium bowl. Spoon 1 cup sauce onto bottom of covered 3-quart casserole; set aside. Reserve remaining sauce.

2. Slice each chicken breast in half crosswise to make 8 thin pieces. Using meat mallet, pound each piece to ¼-inch thickness.

3. Place prosciutto slice (fold in half to fit), 1 roasted pepper half and 1 tablespoon cheese on each piece of chicken. Roll up starting from longer side. Place rolls seam sides down in prepared casserole. Pour reserved sauce over chicken.

4. Cover and bake 50 minutes or until chicken is no longer pink in center. Sprinkle with remaining ½ cup cheese. Bake, uncovered, 10 minutes or until cheese is melted. Slice chicken rolls; serve with sauce over spaghetti.

Makes 4 servings

chicken parmesan

2 cups tomato sauce
1 egg
$^3/_4$ cup plain dry bread crumbs
$^1/_2$ cup grated Parmesan cheese
$^1/_4$ teaspoon salt
$^1/_4$ teaspoon black pepper
1$^1/_2$ pounds chicken tenders (about 12 tenders)
3 tablespoons olive oil
8 ounces fresh mozzarella cheese, cut into thin slices

1. Preheat broiler. Spread tomato sauce evenly in 13×9-inch baking pan.

2. Beat egg in shallow dish. Combine bread crumbs, Parmesan, salt and pepper in another shallow dish.

3. Dip chicken tenders into egg, turning to coat; shake off excess. Dip tenders into crumb mixture, turning to coat.

4. Heat oil in large nonstick skillet over medium-high heat. Cook half the breaded chicken about 5 minutes or until golden brown, turning once. Repeat with remaining chicken.

5. Arrange chicken in single layer on tomato sauce. Top with mozzarella slices. Broil 6 inches from heat 5 to 7 minutes or until cheese is melted and beginning to brown.   *Makes 4 servings*

Tip: To keep your hands from becoming breaded too, use one hand to dip the chicken pieces into the egg and the other hand to coat them with the crumbs.

meaty mushroom spaghetti

2 tablespoons olive oil, divided
1 cup chopped onion
2 cloves garlic, minced
1 pound beef top sirloin, cut into $\frac{1}{2}$-inch cubes
8 ounces sliced fresh mushrooms
1 cup chopped green and yellow bell peppers
1 jar (26 ounces) pasta sauce
1 cup canned diced tomatoes
2 teaspoons dried basil
1 teaspoon dried oregano
16 ounces uncooked spaghetti
    Salt and black pepper
    Grated Parmesan cheese

1. Heat 1 tablespoon oil in large skillet over medium heat. Add onion and garlic; cook and stir until onion is tender. Add beef; cook and stir until browned. Add remaining 1 tablespoon oil, mushrooms and bell peppers; cook and stir 2 minutes. Stir in pasta sauce, tomatoes, basil and oregano. Cover; simmer 15 to 20 minutes, stirring occasionally.

2. Meanwhile, cook spaghetti according to package directions just until al dente; drain well.

3. Combine hot spaghetti and meat sauce in serving bowl; toss lightly. Season with salt and pepper; sprinkle with cheese. Serve immediately.

Makes 6 to 8 servings

chicken vesuvio

1 whole chicken (about 4 pounds)
¼ cup olive oil
3 tablespoons lemon juice
4 cloves garlic, minced
3 large baking potatoes
   Salt and lemon pepper

1. Preheat oven to 375°F. Place chicken, breast side down, on rack in large shallow roasting pan. Combine olive oil, lemon juice and garlic; brush half of oil mixture over chicken. Reserve remaining oil mixture. Roast chicken, uncovered, 30 minutes.

2. Meanwhile, peel potatoes; cut lengthwise into quarters. Turn chicken breast side up. Arrange potatoes around chicken in roasting pan. Brush chicken and potatoes with remaining oil mixture; season with salt and lemon pepper.

3. Roast chicken and potatoes, basting occasionally with pan juices, 50 minutes or until meat thermometer inserted into thickest part of thigh, not touching bone, registers 180°F and potatoes are tender.

Makes 4 to 6 servings

veal piccata with fennel

8 thin veal cutlets or veal scaloppine (about 2 ounces each)
$\frac{1}{2}$ teaspoon whole fennel seeds
  Salt and black pepper
$\frac{1}{2}$ cup all-purpose flour
 2 tablespoons olive oil, divided
 2 tablespoons butter, divided
  Juice of 2 lemons
 2 tablespoons white wine
 2 tablespoons chopped fresh parsley
  Lemon wedges (optional)
  Hot cooked orzo

1. Pound veal between sheets of waxed paper with meat mallet to $\frac{1}{8}$-inch thickness.

2. Crush fennel seeds in mortar with pestle. Or, place seeds in small resealable food storage bag. Squeeze out excess air; seal bag tightly. Crush with rolling pin or wooden mallet.

3. Sprinkle one side of each veal cutlet with crushed fennel seeds; season with salt and pepper. Place flour in shallow bowl. Lightly coat veal pieces with flour.

4. Heat 1 tablespoon each oil and butter in large skillet over medium-high heat until butter is bubbly. Add half of floured veal; cook about 1 minute per side or until veal is tender. Drain well on paper towels. Repeat with remaining oil, butter and floured veal. (Do not drain skillet.)

5. Combine lemon juice and wine in small bowl. Pour juice mixture into skillet to deglaze skillet. Cook over medium-high heat, scraping up any browned bits and stirring frequently.

6. Return veal to skillet; sprinkle with parsley and heat through. Transfer veal and sauce to warm plates. Garnish with lemon. Serve with orzo.

Makes 4 servings

Fish and Seafood

primavera sauce
with artichokes and shrimp

2 tablespoons olive oil
1 cup diced carrots
1 cup diced celery
1 small onion, diced
3 cloves garlic, finely chopped
1 can (28 ounces) CONTADINA® Recipe Ready Crushed Tomatoes
    with Italian Herbs
$1/2$ teaspoon salt
$1/4$ teaspoon black pepper
8 ounces medium raw shrimp, peeled and deveined
1 cup sliced artichoke hearts, drained
Fresh chopped basil (optional)

1. Heat oil in large skillet over high heat. Add carrots, celery, onion and garlic. Cook for 4 to 5 minutes or until carrots are crisp-tender.

2. Add crushed tomatoes, salt and pepper. Bring to boil. Add shrimp and artichoke hearts. Cook for 2 to 3 minutes or until shrimp turn pink.

3. Reduce heat to low; simmer for 2 minutes to blend flavors. Sprinkle with basil. Serve over hot cooked pasta or rice, if desired.

Makes 6 servings

gremolata-crusted salmon fillets

2 slices 7-grain bread
$1/4$ cup loosely packed flat-leaf parsley
1 teaspoon chopped garlic
$1/4$ teaspoon finely grated lemon peel
$1/4$ teaspoon salt
$1/8$ teaspoon ground black pepper
$1/2$ cup HELLMANN'S® or BEST FOODS® Canola Real Mayonnaise
4 salmon fillets (about 4 to 6 ounces each)

1. Preheat oven to 425°F.

2. In food processor, process bread until small crumbs form. Add parsley, garlic, lemon peel, salt and pepper; process until blended. Add Hellmann's or Best Foods Canola Real Mayonnaise and process just until blended. Evenly spread top of each fillet with mayonnaise mixture.

3. On baking sheets or broiler pan, arrange fillets. Bake 15 minutes or until salmon flakes easily with fork.   *Makes 4 servings*

cioppino

1 teaspoon olive oil
1 large onion, chopped
1 cup sliced celery (with celery tops)
1 clove garlic, minced
4 cups water
1 tablespoon Italian seasoning
1 fish-flavored bouillon cube
¼ pound cod or other boneless mild-flavored fish fillets
1 large tomato, chopped
1 can (10 ounces) baby clams, rinsed and drained (optional)
¼ pound small raw shrimp, peeled and deveined
¼ pound raw bay scallops
¼ cup flaked crabmeat or crabmeat blend
2 tablespoons fresh lemon juice

1. Heat olive oil in large saucepan over medium heat until hot. Add onion, celery and garlic. Cook and stir 5 minutes or until onion is soft. Add water, Italian seasoning and bouillon cube. Cover; bring to a boil over high heat.

2. Cut fish into ½-inch pieces. Add fish and tomato to saucepan. Reduce heat to medium-low; simmer about 5 minutes or until fish is opaque. Add clams, if desired, shrimp, scallops, crabmeat and lemon juice; simmer about 5 minutes or until shrimp and scallops are opaque.   *Makes 4 servings*

quick pasta puttanesca

1 package (16 ounces) uncooked spaghetti or linguine
3 tablespoons plus 1 teaspoon olive oil, divided
$^1/_4$ to 1 teaspoon red pepper flakes*
2 cans (6 ounces each) chunk light tuna packed in water, drained
1 tablespoon dried minced onion
1 teaspoon minced garlic
1 can (28 ounces) diced tomatoes
1 can (8 ounces) tomato sauce
24 pitted kalamata or ripe olives
2 tablespoons capers, drained

*For a mildly spicy dish, use $^1/_4$ teaspoon red pepper flakes. For a very spicy dish, use 1 teaspoon red pepper flakes.

1. Cook spaghetti according to package directions; drain. Return spaghetti to saucepan. Add 1 teaspoon oil; toss to coat.

2. Meanwhile, heat remaining 3 tablespoons oil in large skillet over medium-high heat. Add red pepper flakes; cook and stir 1 to 2 minutes or until sizzling. Add tuna; cook and stir 2 to 3 minutes. Add onion and garlic; cook and stir 1 minute. Add tomatoes, tomato sauce, olives and capers. Cook over medium-high heat, stirring frequently, until sauce is heated through.

3. Add sauce to pasta; mix well. *Makes 6 to 8 servings*

swordfish messina style

2 tablespoons olive or vegetable oil
$^1\!/_2$ cup chopped fresh parsley
2 tablespoons chopped fresh basil *or* 2 teaspoons dried basil leaves, crushed
2 cloves garlic, minced
1 can (8 ounces) CONTADINA® Tomato Sauce
$^3\!/_4$ cup sliced fresh mushrooms
1 tablespoon capers
1 tablespoon lemon juice
$^1\!/_8$ teaspoon black pepper
3 pounds swordfish or halibut steaks

1. Heat oil in small saucepan. Add parsley, basil and garlic; sauté for 1 minute. Reduce heat to low. Add tomato sauce, mushrooms and capers; simmer, uncovered, for 5 minutes.

2. Stir in lemon juice and pepper. Place swordfish in single layer in greased 13×9-inch baking dish; cover with sauce.

3. Bake in preheated 400°F oven for 20 minutes or until fish flakes easily when tested with fork. *Makes 8 servings*

orange-glazed roasted salmon and fennel

2 to 3 navel oranges
1 tablespoon FILIPPO BERIO® Extra-Virgin or Pure Olive Oil,
  plus some for the baking pan
1½ teaspoons salt
2 large bulbs fennel
1 large salmon fillet (2 to 2½ pounds)

Preheat the oven to 400°F. Coat a 16×10-inch baking pan with oil.

Grate 1 tablespoon orange zest. Squeeze oranges to get ½ cup juice. In a small bowl whisk the zest, juice, oil, and salt. Trim the fennel. Mince about 2 tablespoons of the feathery leaves; set aside. (The remaining leaves may be reserved for salads or other recipes.) Cut bulbs lengthwise into quarters. Cut out and discard the cores. Cut the fennel into thick slices. Place the fennel in the baking pan. Drizzle with half of the juice mixture. Toss to coat.

Place in the oven for about 20 minutes, stirring occasionally, or until lightly browned. Remove the pan from the oven. Clear a space in the center and lay the salmon diagonally in the pan, skin side down. Drizzle with the remaining juice mixture. Spread to coat the fish. Place in the oven and roast for about 15 minutes, or until the salmon is opaque in the center.

Makes 4 to 6 servings

shrimp scampi

$^1/_3$ cup melted or clarified butter*
2 to 4 tablespoons minced garlic
$1^1/_2$ pounds large raw shrimp, peeled and deveined
6 green onions, thinly sliced
$^1/_4$ cup dry white wine
2 tablespoons lemon juice
8 large sprigs fresh parsley, finely chopped
Salt and black pepper
Lemon wedges (optional)

To clarify butter, melt butter over low heat. Skim off white foam that forms on top, then strain clear golden butter through cheesecloth. Discard milky residue at bottom of pan. Clarified butter will keep, covered, in the refrigerator for up to 2 months.

1. Heat butter in large skillet over medium heat. Add garlic; cook and stir 1 to 2 minutes or until soft but not brown. Add shrimp, green onions, wine and lemon juice; cook 2 to 4 minutes or until shrimp turn pink and opaque, stirring occasionally. *Do not overcook.*

2. Add parsley; season with salt and pepper. Garnish with lemon.

Makes 4 to 6 servings

grilled swordfish sicilian style

3 tablespoons extra-virgin olive oil
1 clove garlic, minced
2 tablespoons lemon juice
³/₄ teaspoon salt
¹/₈ teaspoon black pepper
3 tablespoons capers, drained
1 tablespoon chopped fresh oregano or basil
1¹/₂ pounds swordfish steaks (³/₄ inch thick)

1. Oil grid. Prepare grill for direct cooking.

2. For sauce, heat olive oil in small saucepan over low heat; add garlic. Cook 1 minute. Remove from heat; cool slightly. Whisk in lemon juice, salt and pepper until salt is dissolved. Stir in capers and oregano.

3. Place swordfish on grid over medium heat. Grill 7 to 8 minutes, turning once, or until center is opaque. Serve fish with sauce.

Makes 4 to 6 servings

When cooking fish on the grill, be sure to oil the grid before heating the grill or use a basket especially designed for cooking fish. The basket makes it easy to turn the fish and also helps prevent delicate fish from breaking apart on the grill.

tuna steaks with tomatoes & olives

2 teaspoons olive oil
1 small onion, quartered and sliced
1 clove garlic, minced
$1\frac{1}{3}$ cups chopped tomatoes
$\frac{1}{4}$ cup sliced drained black olives
2 anchovy fillets, finely chopped (optional)
2 tablespoons chopped fresh basil
$\frac{1}{4}$ teaspoon salt, divided
$\frac{1}{8}$ teaspoon red pepper flakes
4 tuna steaks ($\frac{3}{4}$ inch thick)
Black pepper
Nonstick cooking spray
$\frac{1}{4}$ cup toasted pine nuts (optional)

1. Heat oil in large skillet over medium heat. Add onion; cook and stir 4 minutes. Add garlic; cook and stir about 30 seconds. Add tomatoes; cook 3 minutes, stirring occasionally. Stir in olives, anchovy fillets, if desired, basil, $\frac{1}{8}$ teaspoon salt and red pepper flakes. Cook until most of liquid is evaporated.

2. Meanwhile, sprinkle tuna with remaining $\frac{1}{8}$ teaspoon salt and black pepper. Spray large nonstick skillet with cooking spray; heat over medium-high heat. Cook tuna 2 minutes on each side or until medium-rare. Serve with tomato mixture. Garnish with pine nuts. *Makes 4 servings*

fried calamari with tartar sauce

Tartar Sauce (recipe follows)
1 pound cleaned squid (body tubes, tentacles or a combination)
3/4 cup fine dry plain bread crumbs
1 egg
1 tablespoon milk
Vegetable oil
Lemon wedges (optional)

1. Prepare Tartar Sauce; set aside. Rinse squid under cold running water. Cut each squid body tube crosswise into 1/4-inch rings. Pat pieces thoroughly dry with paper towels.

2. Spread bread crumbs on plate. Beat egg with milk in small bowl. Add squid pieces; stir to coat well. Dip squid pieces in bread crumbs; place in shallow bowl or on waxed paper. Let stand 10 to 15 minutes before frying.

3. Heat 1 1/2 inches oil in large saucepan to 350°F. (Caution: Squid will pop and spatter during frying; do not stand too close to pan.) Fry 8 to 10 pieces of squid at a time 45 seconds until light brown. Adjust heat to maintain temperature. Remove with slotted spoon; drain on paper towels. Repeat with remaining squid pieces. *Do not overcook squid or it will become tough.*

4. Serve hot with Tartar Sauce and lemon.   *Makes 2 to 3 servings*

tartar sauce

1 1/3 cups mayonnaise
2 tablespoons chopped fresh parsley
1 small sweet gherkin or pickle, minced
1 tablespoon drained capers, minced
1 green onion, thinly sliced

Combine all ingredients; mix well. Cover; refrigerate until serving time.
                                        Makes about 1 1/3 cups

swordfish pomodoro

1½ pounds swordfish steaks (¾ inch thick)
    Salt and black pepper
  2 tablespoons all-purpose flour
  2 teaspoons olive oil
  1 medium onion, halved and cut into thin slices
  1 clove garlic, minced
1½ cups chopped seeded tomatoes
  ⅓ cup drained mild giardiniera*
  2 tablespoons dry white wine (optional)
  1 tablespoon chopped fresh oregano *or* 1 teaspoon dried oregano
  2 tablespoons canola oil

Giardiniera is an Italian term for pickled vegetables. Available mild or hot, you can find giardiniera in the pickle or ethnic foods section of the supermarket.

1. Sprinkle fish with ⅛ teaspoon salt and pepper. Dredge fish in flour, shaking off excess; set aside.

2. Heat olive oil in medium skillet over medium heat. Add onion; cook and stir 4 minutes or until tender. Add garlic; cook and stir 30 seconds. Add tomatoes; cook 3 minutes, stirring occasionally. Stir in giardiniera, wine, if desired, oregano and ¼ teaspoon salt. Cook 3 minutes or until most liquid is evaporated.

3. Meanwhile, heat canola oil in large nonstick skillet over medium-high heat. Cook fish 4 minutes; turn and cook 3 to 4 minutes or until fish begins to flake when tested with fork. Serve tomato mixture over fish.

Makes 6 servings

seafood marinara with linguine

1 pound dry linguine
2 tablespoons olive or vegetable oil, divided
1 cup chopped onion
3 cloves garlic, minced
1 can (14$\frac{1}{2}$ ounces) CONTADINA® Recipe Ready Diced Tomatoes, undrained
1 can (14$\frac{1}{2}$ ounces) chicken broth
1 can (12 ounces) CONTADINA Tomato Paste
$\frac{1}{2}$ cup dry red wine or water
1 tablespoon chopped fresh basil *or* 2 teaspoons dried basil leaves, crushed
2 teaspoons chopped fresh oregano *or* $\frac{1}{2}$ teaspoon dried oregano leaves, crushed
1 teaspoon salt
8 ounces fresh or frozen medium shrimp, peeled, deveined
8 ounces fresh or frozen bay scallops

1. Cook pasta according to package directions; drain and keep warm.

2. Meanwhile, heat 1 tablespoon oil in large skillet. Add onion and garlic; sauté for 2 minutes.

3. Add undrained tomatoes, broth, tomato paste, wine, basil, oregano and salt. Bring to a boil. Reduce heat to low; simmer, uncovered, for 10 minutes.

4. Heat remaining 1 tablespoon oil in small skillet. Add shrimp and scallops; sauté for 3 to 4 minutes or until shrimp turn pink.

5. Add to sauce; simmer for 2 to 3 minutes or until heated through. Serve over pasta. *Makes 6 servings*

Fish and Seafood

194

rosemary-garlic scallops with polenta

2 teaspoons olive oil
1 medium red bell pepper, sliced
$\frac{1}{3}$ cup chopped red onion
3 cloves garlic, minced
$\frac{1}{2}$ pound fresh bay scallops
2 teaspoons chopped fresh rosemary *or* $\frac{3}{4}$ teaspoon dried rosemary
$\frac{1}{4}$ teaspoon black pepper
1$\frac{1}{4}$ cups chicken broth
$\frac{1}{2}$ cup cornmeal
$\frac{1}{4}$ teaspoon salt

1. Heat oil in large nonstick skillet over medium heat. Add bell pepper, onion and garlic. Cook and stir 5 minutes. Add scallops, rosemary and black pepper. Cook 3 to 5 minutes or until scallops are opaque, stirring occasionally.

2. Meanwhile, combine broth, cornmeal and salt in small saucepan. Bring to a boil over high heat. Reduce heat to low; simmer 5 minutes or until polenta is very thick, stirring frequently. Transfer to serving plates. Top polenta with scallop mixture. *Makes 2 servings*

Fish and Seafood

linguine with red clam sauce

1 tablespoon olive oil
1 onion, finely chopped
2 cloves garlic, minced
2 tablespoons finely chopped fresh parsley
2 teaspoons dried oregano
1 can (about 14 ounces) Italian plum tomatoes, coarsely chopped
1 can (8 ounces) tomato sauce
2 cans ($7\frac{1}{2}$ ounces each) baby clams, undrained
1 tablespoon lemon juice
   Salt and black pepper
8 ounces linguine, cooked and kept warm

1. Heat oil in large saucepan over medium heat until hot. Add onion and garlic; cook and stir about 3 minutes or until tender. Stir in parsley and oregano; cook 1 to 2 minutes.

2. Add tomatoes and tomato sauce to saucepan; bring to a boil. Reduce heat and simmer, uncovered, about 10 minutes or until mixture is slightly thickened. Stir in clams and lemon juice; cook about 3 minutes or until heated through. Season to taste with salt and pepper.

3. Spoon sauce over linguine in large bowl; toss to coat.

Makes 4 servings

Vegetable
Dishes

eggplant italiano

2 tablespoons olive oil, divided
2 medium onions, halved and thinly sliced
2 stalks celery, cut into 1-inch pieces
1¼ pounds eggplant, cut into 1-inch cubes
1 can (about 14 ounces) diced tomatoes, drained
½ cup pitted black olives, cut crosswise into halves
2 tablespoons balsamic vinegar
1 tablespoon sugar
1 tablespoon drained capers
1 teaspoon dried oregano or basil
Salt and black pepper to taste

1. Heat large skillet over medium-high heat 1 minute or until hot. Add 1 tablespoon oil to skillet; heat 30 seconds. Add onions and celery; cook and stir about 2 minutes or until tender. Remove; set aside. Reduce heat to medium.

2. Add remaining 1 tablespoon oil to skillet; heat 30 seconds. Add eggplant; cook and stir about 4 minutes or until tender. Add tomatoes and reserved onion mixture; mix well. Cover; cook 10 minutes.

3. Stir olives, vinegar, sugar, capers and oregano into eggplant mixture. Season with salt and pepper. *Makes 6 servings*

Vegetable Dishes

lasagna florentine

2 tablespoons olive oil
3 carrots, finely chopped
1 package (8 ounces) sliced mushrooms
1 medium onion, finely chopped
2 cloves garlic, minced
1 jar (1 pound 10 ounces) RAGÚ® Robusto® Pasta Sauce
1 container (15 ounces) ricotta cheese
2 cups (8 ounces) shredded mozzarella cheese, divided
1 box (10 ounces) frozen chopped spinach, thawed and squeezed dry
2 eggs
$1/4$ cup grated Parmesan cheese
1 teaspoon salt
1 teaspoon dried Italian seasoning
16 lasagna noodles, cooked and drained

1. Preheat oven to 375°F. In 12-inch skillet, heat olive oil over medium heat. Cook carrots, mushrooms, onion and garlic until carrots are almost tender, about 5 minutes. Stir in Pasta Sauce; heat through.

2. Meanwhile, in medium bowl, combine ricotta cheese, $1\frac{1}{2}$ cups mozzarella cheese, spinach, eggs, Parmesan cheese, salt and Italian seasoning; set aside.

3. In 13×9-inch baking dish, evenly spread $1/2$ cup sauce mixture. Arrange 4 lasagna noodles, lengthwise over sauce, overlapping edges slightly. Spread one third of ricotta mixture over noodles; repeat layers, ending with noodles. Top with remaining sauce and $1/2$ cup mozzarella cheese. Cover with foil and bake 40 minutes. Remove foil and continue baking 10 minutes or until bubbling. *Makes 8 servings*

Vegetable Dishes

italian tomato bake

1 pound sweet Italian sausage, cut into $1/2$-inch slices
2 tablespoons butter
1 cup chopped onion
4 cups cooked egg noodles
2 cups frozen broccoli florets, thawed and drained
2 cups prepared pasta sauce
$1/2$ cup diced plum tomatoes
2 cloves garlic, minced
3 plum tomatoes, sliced
1 cup (8 ounces) ricotta cheese
$1/3$ cup grated Parmesan cheese
1 teaspoon dried oregano

1. Preheat oven to 350°F. Cook sausage in large skillet over medium heat about 10 minutes or until barely pink in center. Drain on paper towels; set aside. Drain fat from skillet.

2. Add butter and onion to skillet; cook and stir until onion is tender. Combine onion, noodles, broccoli, pasta sauce, diced tomatoes and garlic in large bowl; mix well. Transfer to 13×9-inch baking dish.

3. Top with cooked sausage; place tomato slices on top. Place 1 heaping tablespoonful ricotta cheese on each tomato slice. Sprinkle with Parmesan cheese and oregano. Bake 35 minutes or until hot and bubbly.

Makes 6 servings

broccoli italian style

1¼ pounds broccoli
2 tablespoons lemon juice
2 teaspoons extra-virgin olive oil
1 clove garlic, minced
1 teaspoon chopped fresh parsley
Dash black pepper

1. Trim broccoli, discarding tough stems. Cut broccoli into florets with 2-inch stems. Peel remaining broccoli stems; cut into ½-inch-thick slices.

2. Bring 1 quart water to a boil in large saucepan over high heat. Add broccoli; return to a boil. Reduce heat to medium-high. Cook, uncovered, 3 to 5 minutes or until broccoli is fork-tender. Drain; transfer to serving dish.

3. Combine lemon juice, oil, garlic, parsley and pepper in small bowl. Pour over broccoli; toss to coat. *Makes 4 servings*

Tip

Though grown in Italy for centuries, broccoli didn't become popular until the 1920's in the United States where it is now widely available. Whether steaming or boiling, cook broccoli uncovered to keep its bright green color

grilled asparagus and peppers

$1/2$ cup balsamic vinegar
$1/4$ cup olive oil
 1 tablespoon chopped onion
 1 clove garlic, minced
$1/2$ teaspoon dried basil
$1/2$ teaspoon dried thyme
$1/2$ teaspoon lemon pepper seasoning
$1/4$ teaspoon salt
 1 pound thin asparagus, trimmed
 1 large red bell pepper, cut into $1/2$-inch-wide strips
 1 large yellow bell pepper, cut into $1/2$-inch-wide strips

1. Combine vinegar, oil, onion, garlic, basil, thyme, lemon pepper and salt in small bowl until blended. Place vinegar mixture, asparagus and bell peppers in large resealable food storage bag. Close bag securely, turning to coat. Marinate 30 minutes, turning after 15 minutes.

2. Prepare grill for direct cooking.

3. Drain asparagus and bell peppers; reserve marinade. Grill over medium-high heat 8 to 10 minutes or until tender, turning halfway through grilling time and brushing frequently with reserved marinade. Serve hot or at room temperature.

Makes 5 to 6 servings

sautéed swiss chard

1 large bunch Swiss chard or kale (about 1 pound)
1 tablespoon olive oil
3 cloves garlic, minced
$\frac{3}{4}$ teaspoon salt
$\frac{1}{4}$ teaspoon black pepper
1 tablespoon balsamic vinegar (optional)
$\frac{1}{4}$ cup pine nuts, toasted

1. Rinse chard in cold water; shake off excess water but do not dry. Finely chop stems and coarsely chop leaves.

2. Heat oil in large saucepan or Dutch oven over medium heat. Add garlic; cook and stir 2 minutes. Add chard, salt and pepper. Cover and cook 2 minutes or until chard begins to wilt. Uncover; cook and stir about 5 minutes or until chard is evenly wilted.

3. Stir in vinegar, if desired. Just before serving, sprinkle with pine nuts.

Makes 4 servings

Chard is a tall leafy green vegetable with a thick, crunchy stalk that comes in white, red or yellow with wide fan-like green leaves. Both the leaves and stalk of chard are edible, although the stems vary in texture with the white ones being the most tender. Chard has the bitterness of beet greens and the slightly salty flavor of spinach leaves

vegetable frittata

4½ teaspoons olive oil, divided
¼ cup chopped onion
6 eggs
1 package (10 ounces) frozen chopped spinach, thawed, well drained
¾ cup (3 ounces) shredded Cheddar cheese
½ teaspoon salt
⅛ teaspoon black pepper
Dash ground red pepper
Dash ground nutmeg

1. Heat 3 teaspoons olive oil in large nonstick skillet over medium heat. Add onion; cook until tender, stirring occasionally. Remove onion from skillet with slotted spoon; set aside.

2. Lightly beat eggs in medium bowl. Add onion, spinach, cheese and seasonings.

3. Heat remaining 1½ teaspoons oil in same skillet. Add egg mixture. Cook 5 minutes or until bottom is lightly browned.

4. Place large plate over frittata. Invert frittata onto plate. Slide frittata, uncooked side down, back into skillet.

5. Continue cooking 4 minutes or until set. Cut into wedges to serve. Garnish, if desired.   *Makes 4 to 6 servings*

fennel braised with tomato

2 bulbs fennel
1 tablespoon olive oil
1 small onion, sliced
1 clove garlic, sliced
4 medium tomatoes, chopped
$^2/_3$ cup vegetable broth or water
3 tablespoons dry white wine or vegetable broth
1 teaspoon dried marjoram *or* 1 tablespoon chopped fresh marjoram
$^1/_4$ teaspoon salt
$^1/_4$ teaspoon black pepper

1. Trim stems and bottoms from fennel bulbs; reserve green leafy tops for garnish. Cut each bulb lengthwise into 4 wedges.

2. Heat oil in large skillet over medium heat. Cook fennel, onion and garlic, stirring occasionally, until onion is soft and translucent, about 5 minutes.

3. Add tomatoes, broth, wine and marjoram. Season with salt and pepper. Cover; simmer gently until fennel is tender, about 20 minutes. Garnish with fennel tops. *Makes 6 servings*

Vegetable Dishes

grilled tricolored pepper salad

1 each large red, yellow and green bell pepper, cut into halves or quarters
¹/₃ cup extra-virgin olive oil
3 tablespoons balsamic vinegar
2 cloves garlic, minced
¹/₄ teaspoon salt
¹/₄ teaspoon black pepper
¹/₃ cup crumbled goat cheese (about 1¹/₂ ounces)
¹/₄ cup thinly sliced fresh basil leaves

1. Prepare grill for direct cooking.

2. Place bell peppers, skin-side down, on grid. Grill bell peppers, covered, over hot coals 10 to 12 minutes or until skin is charred. Place charred peppers in paper bag. Close bag; set aside 10 to 15 minutes. Remove skin with paring knife; discard skin.

3. Place bell peppers in shallow glass serving dish. Combine oil, vinegar, garlic, salt and black pepper in small bowl; whisk until well combined. Pour over bell peppers. Let stand 30 minutes at room temperature. (Or, cover and refrigerate up to 24 hours. Bring bell peppers to room temperature before serving.)

4. Sprinkle peppers with cheese and basil just before serving.

Makes 4 to 6 servings

eggplant parmigiana

2 eggs, beaten
$\frac{1}{4}$ cup milk
  Dash garlic powder
  Dash onion powder
  Dash salt
  Dash black pepper
$\frac{1}{2}$ cup seasoned dry bread crumbs
1 large eggplant, cut into $\frac{1}{2}$-inch-thick slices
  Vegetable oil for frying
1 jar (about 26 ounces) pasta sauce
4 cups (16 ounces) shredded mozzarella cheese
$2\frac{1}{2}$ cups (10 ounces) shredded Swiss cheese
$\frac{1}{4}$ cup grated Parmesan cheese
$\frac{1}{4}$ cup grated Romano cheese

1. Preheat oven to 350°F. Combine eggs, milk, garlic powder, onion powder, salt and pepper in shallow dish. Place bread crumbs in another shallow dish. Dip eggplant into egg mixture; coat in bread crumbs.

2. Heat $\frac{1}{4}$ inch oil in large skillet over medium-high heat. Brown eggplant on both sides in batches; drain on paper towels.

3. Cover bottom of 13×9-inch baking dish with 3 tablespoons pasta sauce. Layer half of eggplant, half of mozzarella cheese, half of Swiss cheese and half of remaining sauce in dish. Repeat layers. Sprinkle with Parmesan and Romano cheeses.

4. Bake 30 minutes or until heated through and cheeses are melted.

Makes 4 servings

artichokes with dijon mayonnaise

2 DOLE® Fresh Artichokes
Lemon juice
$^2/_3$ cup fat-free or reduced-fat mayonnaise
2 tablespoons finely chopped DOLE® Green Onions
1 tablespoon lemon juice
1 tablespoon Dijon-style mustard
$^1/_4$ teaspoon prepared horseradish

• Wash artichokes; trim stems. Cut off 1 inch from tops of artichokes; cut off sharp leaf tips. Brush cut edges with lemon juice to prevent browning.

• Place artichokes in large pot of boiling water (artichokes should be completely covered with water).

• Cook, covered, 25 to 35 minutes or until leaf pulls off easily from artichoke. Drain artichokes upside down 10 to 15 minutes.

• Stir together mayonnaise, green onions, 1 tablespoon lemon juice, mustard and horseradish in small bowl.

• Spoon dip into serving bowl; serve with artichokes.

Makes 6 servings

Curry Mayonnaise: Omit mustard; stir in 2 teaspoons curry powder and 1 teaspoon chutney.

Garlic Mayonnaise: Omit mustard; stir in 2 garlic cloves, minced, and 2 tablespoons fresh minced parsley.

Herb Mayonnaise: Omit mustard; stir in 2 tablespoons nonfat milk and $^1/_2$ teaspoon each: dill weed, dried basil leaves, crushed and dried rosemary, crushed.

risi bisi

1½ cups uncooked converted long-grain rice
¾ cup chopped onion
2 cloves garlic, minced
2 cans (about 14 ounces each) chicken broth
⅓ cup water
¾ teaspoon Italian seasoning
½ teaspoon dried basil
½ cup frozen peas
¼ cup grated Parmesan cheese
¼ cup toasted pine nuts (optional)

Slow Cooker Directions

1. Combine rice, onion and garlic in slow cooker.

2. Bring broth and water to a boil in small saucepan. Stir broth mixture, Italian seasoning and basil into rice mixture in slow cooker. Cover; cook on LOW 2 to 3 hours or until liquid is absorbed.

3. Add peas. Cover; cook on LOW 1 hour. Stir in cheese. Sprinkle with pine nuts.   *Makes 6 servings*

Tip

Risi Bisi ("rice and peas") is a traditional Italian dish. It is the first dish served each April 29th at the Venetian feasts honoring St. Mark. Small Italian peas are at their most sweet and tender at that time of year.

oven roasted tomatoes

6 ripe plum or vine tomatoes
2 cloves garlic, crushed
1 teaspoon dried oregano
   Salt and freshly ground black pepper
5 tablespoons FILIPPO BERIO® Olive Oil

Preheat the oven to 375°F. Cut the tomatoes in half and place cut side up in a single layer, in a large oven-proof dish. Scatter tomatoes with the oregano, garlic and plenty of seasoning, then drizzle with oil. Bake for 30 to 35 minutes or until the tomatoes have softened. Delicious served with roast chicken. *Makes 4 servings*

Slow roasting tomatoes gives the tomatoes a sweeter and more savory flavor. Serve them as antipasti, a side dish or use to make a rich tomato sauce.

fennel with black olive dressing

1¹/₄ pounds (about 2 medium-size heads) fennel
¹/₃ cup lemon juice
¹/₄ cup olive or salad oil
²/₃ cup pitted California ripe olives, coarsely chopped
   Salt and pepper

Trim stems and root ends from fennel; core. Reserve feathery wisps of fennel for garnish, if desired. Slice fennel crosswise into ¹/₄-inch-thick pieces. In 4- to 5-quart pan, bring 3 to 4 quarts water to a boil over high heat. Add fennel and cook, uncovered, just until tender to bite, about 5 minutes. Drain; immerse fennel in ice water until cold. Drain well again. In small bowl, whisk lemon juice and oil; stir in olives and add salt and pepper to taste. To serve, divide fennel among 6 salad plates and spoon dressing over fennel. Garnish with reserved feathery wisps of fennel, if desired.

Makes 6 servings

Favorite recipe from **California Olive Industry**

oven-roasted potatoes with rosemary

4 medium all-purpose potatoes (about 2 pounds), peeled, if desired, and cut into large chunks

6 tablespoons I CAN'T BELIEVE IT'S NOT BUTTER!® Spread, melted

1 large shallot or small onion, thinly sliced

2 teaspoons chopped fresh rosemary leaves *or* $\frac{1}{2}$ teaspoon dried rosemary leaves, crushed

$\frac{3}{4}$ teaspoon salt

$\frac{1}{8}$ teaspoon ground black pepper

Preheat oven to 450°F.

In large bowl, combine all ingredients. In 13×9-inch baking or roasting pan, arrange potato mixture. Roast, stirring occasionally, 50 minutes or until potatoes are tender and golden.   *Makes 4 servings*

Add carrots, sweet potatoes and/or onions, cut into large chunks, to the potatoes for an easy way to put fabulous tasting vegetables on the table.

italian alfredo broccoli strata

1 loaf (12 ounces) Italian bread, cut into 1-inch cubes
1 jar (1 pound) RAGÚ® Cheesy! Classic Alfredo Sauce
3 cups milk
6 eggs, lightly beaten
1½ cups shredded mozzarella cheese (about 6 ounces)
1 box (10 ounces) frozen chopped broccoli, thawed and drained

1. Preheat oven to 350°F. In greased 13×9-inch baking dish, arrange bread cubes; set aside.

2. In large bowl with wire whisk, combine remaining ingredients; pour over bread. Let stand 1 hour or cover and refrigerate overnight.

3. Bake uncovered, 45 minutes or until center is set.   *Makes 6 servings*

Variation: For a meat variation, add 1 cup coarsely diced cooked ham, 1 cup crumbled cooked sausage or 6 slices bacon, cooked and crumbled.

Italian *Sweets*

classic anise biscotti

$^3/_4$ cup (about 4 ounces) whole blanched almonds
2$^1/_4$ cups all-purpose flour
1 teaspoon baking powder
$^3/_4$ teaspoon salt
$^3/_4$ cup sugar
$^1/_2$ cup (1 stick) unsalted butter, softened
3 eggs
2 tablespoons brandy
2 teaspoons grated lemon peel
1 tablespoon anise seeds

1. Preheat oven to 375°F. Spread almonds in single layer on ungreased baking sheet. Bake 6 to 8 minutes or until lightly browned; turn off oven. Let almonds cool slightly; coarsely chop.

2. Combine flour, baking powder and salt in small bowl. Beat sugar and butter in medium bowl with electric mixer at medium speed until light and fluffy. Add eggs, one at a time, beating well after each addition. Stir in brandy and lemon peel. Gradually add flour mixture, stirring until smooth. Stir in almonds and anise seeds. Cover; refrigerate dough 1 hour or until firm.

3. Preheat oven to 375°F. Grease baking sheet. Divide dough in half. Shape each half of dough into 12×2-inch log on lightly floured surface. (Dough will be fairly soft.) Pat smooth with lightly floured fingertips. Transfer to prepared baking sheet. Bake 20 to 25 minutes or until logs are light golden brown. *Reduce oven temperature to 350°F.* Cool logs on wire rack.

4. Cut logs diagonally with serrated knife into $^1/_2$-inch-thick slices. Place slices flat in single layer on ungreased baking sheets.

5. Bake 8 minutes. Turn slices; bake 10 to 12 minutes or until cut surfaces are lightly browned and biscotti are dry. Remove cookies to wire racks; cool completely. Store biscotti in airtight container up to 2 weeks.

Makes about 4 dozen cookies

rustic honey polenta cake

$2\frac{1}{2}$ cups all-purpose flour
1 cup yellow cornmeal
2 tablespoons baking powder
1 teaspoon salt
1 cup (2 sticks) butter or margarine, melted
$1\frac{3}{4}$ cups milk
$\frac{3}{4}$ cup honey
2 eggs, slightly beaten
Honey-Orange Syrup (recipe follows)
Sweetened whipped cream and orange segments for garnish
(optional)

In large bowl, combine flour, cornmeal, baking powder and salt; mix well. In small bowl, combine melted butter, milk, honey and eggs; mix well. Stir into flour mixture, mixing until just blended. Pour into lightly greased 13×9-inch baking pan.

Bake at 325°F for 25 to 30 minutes or until toothpick comes out clean. Meanwhile, prepare Honey-Orange Syrup. When cake is done, remove from oven to wire rack. Pour hot syrup evenly over top of cake, spreading if necessary to cover entire surface. Cool completely. Garnish with dollop of whipped cream and orange segments, if desired.   *Makes 12 servings*

Honey-Orange Syrup: In small saucepan, whisk together $\frac{1}{2}$ cup honey, 3 tablespoons orange juice concentrate and 1 tablespoon freshly grated orange peel. Heat over medium-high heat until mixture begins to boil; remove from heat.

Favorite recipe from **National Honey Board**

Italian Sweets

italian ice

1 cup sugar
1 cup sweet or dry fruity white wine
1 cup water
1 cup lemon juice
2 egg whites*
    Fresh berries (optional)

*Use pasteurized or clean, uncracked grade A eggs.

1. Combine sugar, wine and water in small saucepan. Cook over medium-high heat until sugar is dissolved and syrup boils, stirring frequently. Cover; boil 1 minute. Uncover; adjust heat to maintain simmer. Simmer 10 minutes without stirring. Remove from heat. Refrigerate 1 hour or until syrup is completely cool.

2. Stir lemon juice into cooled syrup. Pour into 9-inch round cake pan. Freeze 1 hour.

3. Quickly stir mixture with fork breaking up ice crystals. Freeze 1 hour more or until firm but not solid. Meanwhile, place medium bowl in freezer to chill.

4. Beat egg whites in small bowl with electric mixer at high speed until stiff peaks form. Remove lemon mixture from pan to chilled bowl. Immediately beat lemon mixture with whisk or fork until smooth. Fold in egg whites; mix well. Spread mixture evenly into same cake pan. Freeze 30 minutes. Stir with fork; cover pan with foil. Freeze at least 3 hours or until firm.

5. To serve, scoop ice into dessert dishes. Garnish with berries.

Makes 4 servings

grandma's cannoli cassata

6 cups whipping cream
2 eggs
1 cup sugar
1 cup all-purpose flour
1 teaspoon grated lemon peel
$\frac{1}{2}$ cup finely chopped dried fruit
$\frac{1}{2}$ cup ricotta cheese
$\frac{1}{2}$ cup rum
$\frac{1}{4}$ cup chopped pecans
2 teaspoons vanilla
1 pound cake (about 16 ounces), cut into $\frac{1}{2}$-inch cubes

1. Whisk cream and eggs in medium saucepan just until blended. Whisk in sugar, flour and lemon peel until blended. Cook and stir over medium heat 5 to 10 minutes or until mixture begins to thicken. *Do not boil.* Remove from heat; stir in dried fruit, ricotta cheese, rum, pecans and vanilla.

2. Place one third of cake cubes in trifle dish, distributing pieces to cover bottom of bowl. Top with one third of cream mixture. Repeat layers twice, ending with cream mixture. Cover with plastic wrap; refrigerate at least 4 hours or overnight. Garnish as desired. Serve cold.

Makes 12 servings

polenta apricot pudding cake

¼ cup chopped dried apricots
¼ cup water
2 cups orange juice
1 cup ricotta cheese
3 tablespoons honey
¾ cup sugar
½ cup all-purpose flour
½ cup cornmeal
¼ teaspoon ground nutmeg
½ cup slivered almonds
Powdered sugar (optional)

1. Preheat oven to 300°F. Spray 10-inch nonstick springform pan with nonstick cooking spray.

2. Soak apricots in water in small bowl 15 minutes; drain. Pat apricots dry with paper towels; set aside.

3. Combine orange juice, ricotta cheese and honey in medium bowl. Beat with electric mixer at medium speed 5 minutes or until smooth. Combine sugar, flour, cornmeal and nutmeg in small bowl; gradually add to orange juice mixture, blending well. Stir in apricots.

4. Pour batter into prepared pan. Sprinkle with almonds. Bake 60 to 70 minutes or until center is firm and cake is golden brown. Sprinkle with powdered sugar. Serve warm.   *Makes 8 servings*

chocolate espresso panini

2 tablespoons chocolate hazelnut spread
$1/4$ teaspoon instant espresso powder
2 slices rustic Italian bread
Nonstick cooking spray

1. Preheat indoor grill.* Combine chocolate spread and espresso powder in small bowl; mix well. Spread chocolate mixture evenly over one slice bread; top with second slice.

2. Spray sandwich lightly with nonstick cooking spray. Grill 2 to 3 minutes or until bread is golden brown. *Makes 1 panini*

*Panini can also be made on the stove in a ridged grill pan or in a nonstick skillet. Cook sandwich over medium heat about 2 minutes per side.

Panini are "small sandwiches" typically made using a small loaf of ciabatta bread and grilled.

fig and hazelnut cake

$^3/_4$ cup hazelnuts (about 4 ounces) with skins removed, coarsely
    chopped
$^3/_4$ cup whole dried figs (about 4 ounces), coarsely chopped
$^2/_3$ cup slivered blanched almonds (about 3 ounces), coarsely chopped
  3 squares (1 ounce each) semisweet chocolate, finely chopped
$^1/_3$ cup diced candied orange peel
$^1/_3$ cup diced candied lemon peel
$1^1/_4$ cups all-purpose flour
$1^3/_4$ teaspoons baking powder
$^3/_4$ teaspoon salt
  3 eggs
$^1/_2$ cup sugar

1. Preheat oven to 300°F. Grease 8×4-inch loaf pan; set aside. Combine hazelnuts, figs, almonds, chocolate and candied orange and lemon peels in medium bowl; mix well. Combine flour, baking powder and salt in small bowl.

2. Beat eggs and sugar 5 minutes in large bowl with electric mixer at high speed until thick and pale yellow. Gently fold nut mixture into egg mixture. Sift half of flour mixture over egg mixture; gently fold until blended. Repeat with remaining flour mixture.

3. Spread batter evenly in prepared pan. Bake 60 to 70 minutes or until top is golden brown and firm to the touch. Cool in pan on wire rack 5 minutes. Remove loaf from pan; cool completely on wire rack.

Makes 12 servings

orange-scented panna cotta

2 tablespoons orange-flavored liqueur or orange juice
1 envelope unflavored gelatin
3 cups heavy cream
¼ cup powdered sugar
2 tablespoons sucralose-based sugar substitute
1 teaspoon freshly grated orange peel
½ teaspoon vanilla

1. Combine liqueur and gelatin in small bowl. Let stand 10 minutes; do not stir. (Gelatin will absorb liquid.)

2. Combine cream, powdered sugar, sucralose and orange peel in heavy saucepan. Bring to a simmer, stirring constantly, over medium heat. Add gelatin mixture; cook and stir 1 minute or until gelatin is dissolved. Remove from heat; stir in vanilla.

3. Spoon cream mixture into 6 custard cups. Let stand 30 minutes to cool. Refrigerate 3 to 4 hours.

4. Serve panna cotta in custard cups or unmold and invert onto serving plates. *Makes 6 servings*

ginger polenta cookies

$2\frac{1}{4}$ cups all-purpose flour
$\frac{1}{2}$ cup uncooked instant polenta or yellow cornmeal
$\frac{1}{2}$ cup toasted pistachio nuts or pine nuts, finely chopped
$\frac{1}{2}$ cup dried cranberries, finely chopped
    Pinch salt
    1 cup (2 sticks) unsalted butter, softened
$\frac{3}{4}$ cup sugar
    1 egg
    1 egg yolk
$\frac{1}{2}$ cup finely chopped crystallized ginger
$\frac{1}{2}$ teaspoon ground ginger

1. Combine flour, polenta, pistachio nuts, cranberries and salt in medium bowl; set aside.

2. Beat butter and sugar in large bowl with electric mixer at medium speed until light and fluffy. Beat in egg, egg yolk, chopped ginger and ground ginger. Add flour mixture; mix at low speed until well blended.

3. Gather dough into ball; divide in half. Shape into 2 (9-inch) logs; wrap in plastic wrap and seal ends. Roll logs to smooth surface, if necessary. Refrigerate 4 to 6 hours or until firm.

4. Preheat oven to 300°F. Line cookie sheets with parchment paper. Cut logs into $\frac{1}{4}$-inch slices; place cookies on prepared cookie sheets. Bake 15 to 18 minutes or until edges are golden. Cool 2 to 3 minutes on cookie sheets; transfer to wire racks to cool completely.

Makes about 5 dozen cookies

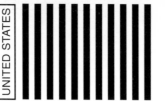

BUSINESS REPLY MAIL

FIRST-CLASS MAIL   PERMIT NO. 24   MT. MORRIS, IL

POSTAGE WILL BE PAID BY ADDRESSEE

EASY HOME COOKING
PO BOX 520
MT MORRIS IL 61054-7451

orange-thyme granita in cookie cups

2$\frac{1}{2}$ cups fresh orange juice
$\frac{1}{2}$ cup fresh lemon juice
$\frac{1}{4}$ cup sugar
1 teaspoon finely chopped fresh thyme
6 Lemon-Anise Cookie Cups (recipe follows)

1. Combine juices, sugar and thyme in medium bowl; stir until sugar dissolves. Freeze about 1 hour or until slightly firm. Beat with wire whisk to break ice crystals. Repeat freezing and beating process 2 to 3 times until ice is firm and granular.

2. Meanwhile, prepare Lemon Anise Cookie Cups. To serve, scoop $\frac{1}{2}$ cup granita into each cookie cup. *Makes 6 servings*

lemon-anise cookie cups

3 tablespoons all-purpose flour
3 tablespoons sugar
2 tablespoons butter, melted
1 egg white
1 teaspoon grated lemon peel
$\frac{1}{4}$ teaspoon anise extract
$\frac{1}{4}$ cup sliced almonds

1. Preheat oven to 375°F. Combine flour, sugar, butter, egg white, lemon peel and anise extract in food processor; process until smooth. Spray outside of bottoms of 6 custard cups and 2 baking sheets with nonstick cooking spray. Spread 1 tablespoon batter into 5-inch-diameter circle on baking sheet with rubber spatula. Repeat to make total of 6 circles. Sprinkle 2 teaspoons almonds in center of each.

2. Bake 3 to 4 minutes or until edges are browned. Place each cookie over bottom of prepared custard cup so almonds face inside. Press cookies against custard cup to form cookie cup. Cool. *Makes 6 cookie cups*

minted pears with gorgonzola

4 whole firm pears with stems, peeled
2 cups Concord grape juice
1 tablespoon honey
1 tablespoon finely chopped fresh mint
1 cinnamon stick
$\frac{1}{4}$ teaspoon ground nutmeg
$\frac{1}{4}$ cup Gorgonzola cheese, crumbled

1. Place pears in medium saucepan. Add grape juice, honey, mint, cinnamon stick and nutmeg. Bring to a boil over high heat. Reduce heat; simmer, covered, 15 to 20 minutes, turning pears once to absorb juices evenly. Cook until pears can be pierced easily with fork. Remove pan from heat; cool. Remove pears with slotted spoon; set aside. Discard cinnamon stick.

2. Bring juice mixture to a boil. Reduce heat and simmer 20 minutes. Place pears on individual serving plates. Pour juice mixture over pears. Sprinkle Gorgonzola evenly around pears. *Makes 4 servings*

Gorgonzola is Italy's version of blue cheese.

Acknowledgments

The publisher would like to thank the companies listed below for the use of their recipes and photographs in this publication.

Birds Eye Foods

California Olive Industry

Del Monte Corporation

Dole Food Company, Inc.

Filippo Berio® Olive Oil

McIlhenny Company (TABASCO® brand Pepper Sauce)

Mushroom Council

National Cattlemen's Beef Association on behalf of The Beef Checkoff

National Honey Board

National Onion Association

Reckitt Benckiser Inc.

Sargento® Foods Inc.

Sonoma® Dried Tomatoes

Unilever

Wisconsin Milk Marketing Board

Index

METRIC CONVERSION CHART

VOLUME MEASUREMENTS (dry)

$1/8$ teaspoon = 0.5 mL
$1/4$ teaspoon = 1 mL
$1/2$ teaspoon = 2 mL
$3/4$ teaspoon = 4 mL
1 teaspoon = 5 mL
1 tablespoon = 15 mL
2 tablespoons = 30 mL
$1/4$ cup = 60 mL
$1/3$ cup = 75 mL
$1/2$ cup = 125 mL
$2/3$ cup = 150 mL
$3/4$ cup = 175 mL
1 cup = 250 mL
2 cups = 1 pint = 500 mL
3 cups = 750 mL
4 cups = 1 quart = 1 L

VOLUME MEASUREMENTS (fluid)

1 fluid ounce (2 tablespoons) = 30 mL
4 fluid ounces ($1/2$ cup) = 125 mL
8 fluid ounces (1 cup) = 250 mL
12 fluid ounces ($1 1/2$ cups) = 375 mL
16 fluid ounces (2 cups) = 500 mL

WEIGHTS (mass)

$1/2$ ounce = 15 g
1 ounce = 30 g
3 ounces = 90 g
4 ounces = 120 g
8 ounces = 225 g
10 ounces = 285 g
12 ounces = 360 g
16 ounces = 1 pound = 450 g

DIMENSIONS

$1/16$ inch = 2 mm
$1/8$ inch = 3 mm
$1/4$ inch = 6 mm
$1/2$ inch = 1.5 cm
$3/4$ inch = 2 cm
1 inch = 2.5 cm

OVEN TEMPERATURES

250°F = 120°C
275°F = 140°C
300°F = 150°C
325°F = 160°C
350°F = 180°C
375°F = 190°C
400°F = 200°C
425°F = 220°C
450°F = 230°C

BAKING PAN SIZES

Utensil	Size in Inches/Quarts	Metric Volume	Size in Centimeters
Baking or Cake Pan (square or rectangular)	$8 \times 8 \times 2$	2 L	$20 \times 20 \times 5$
	$9 \times 9 \times 2$	2.5 L	$23 \times 23 \times 5$
	$12 \times 8 \times 2$	3 L	$30 \times 20 \times 5$
	$13 \times 9 \times 2$	3.5 L	$33 \times 23 \times 5$
Loaf Pan	$8 \times 4 \times 3$	1.5 L	$20 \times 10 \times 7$
	$9 \times 5 \times 3$	2 L	$23 \times 13 \times 7$
Round Layer Cake Pan	$8 \times 1 1/2$	1.2 L	20×4
	$9 \times 1 1/2$	1.5 L	23×4
Pie Plate	$8 \times 1 1/4$	750 mL	20×3
	$9 \times 1 1/4$	1 L	23×3
Baking Dish or Casserole	1 quart	1 L	—
	$1 1/2$ quart	1.5 L	—
	2 quart	2 L	—